JOHN BYNNER & SAMANTHA PARSONS

IT DOESN'T GET ANY BETTER

THE IMPACT OF POOR BASIC SKILLS ON THE LIVES OF 37 YEAR OLDS

It doesn't get any better

The impact of poor basic skills on the lives of 37 year olds

Foreword

It doesn't get any better reports the comprehensive findings of the latest research for the Agency by the Social Statistics Research Unit at City University, based on the National Child Development Study (NCDS). The research looks in detail at adults with poor basic skills, who are part of the group followed since their birth in 1958.

As they reach 'the heart of adult life' it's clear that problems with basic skills have a continuing, adverse, effect on their lives. People with limited basic skills are less likely than those with good basic skills to have a job. Critically, the research shows a widening gap. As jobs require more skills, those with limited skills are increasingly marginalised.

They are less likely to have been promoted or to have had training at work. They are less likely to be a member of a public organisation or to vote in a general election. The evidence in this report gives a stark picture of disadvantage in the labour market and social exclusion. Yet, as the authors point out, it underestimates the gravity of the situation. With all longitudinal surveys the cohort gets smaller over time. Those with good basic skills are more likely to remain, those with poor basic skills are more likely to drop out.

I am grateful to Professor John Bynner and Samantha Parsons for undertaking this research, which extends our knowledge of the problems faced by an often neglected group of people. *It doesn't get any better* gives us important information about the depth of the impact of poor basic skills on adults' home and working lives. It also shows the imperative to change this.

Whilst the proportion of those with literacy or numeracy problems who have been to a class to improve their literacy and numeracy is higher than that in a comparable study of twenty one year olds, it's still low at under 20%. This research reinforces the importance of extending current programmes for those who have usually benefited least from initial education. Basic skills programmes which improve people's chances of getting back into work, and reduce social exclusion, are an urgent priority.

Alan Wells OBE
Director
The Basic Skills Agency

Contents

Tables

Figures

It doesn't get any better
The impact on poor basic skills on the lives of 37 year olds

A summary

The series of studies of basic skills carried out for the Basic Skills Agency (BSA) by the Social Statistics Research Unit (SSRU) at City University have brought to light the disadvantaged circumstances of people with poor literacy or numeracy skills - both self-reported and assessed difficulties - and their origins.

The previous reports (NCDS age 23; BCS70 age 21) have pointed out the consequences of a poor grasp of literacy and numeracy skills. The cycle of disadvantage starting in childhood places a brake on further educational progress and is likely to lead to a wide range of difficulties, often including social exclusion in adult life. The most recent 37 year survey of the NCDS cohort offers the opportunity of examining the effect of basic skills difficulties over 20 years of working and family life, and the transition into mature adulthood and citizenship.

The data gave strong indications that the consequences of poor functional literacy and numeracy inherited from bad education, compound the problems the NCDS cohort members faced as they moved through adulthood. The gap between those with limited literacy and numeracy skills and those with average or good skills was wider on a number of key indicators than found from research conducted at younger ages. People with severe literacy or numeracy difficulties were first identified on the basis of their literacy or numeracy test scores, and the kinds of difficulties they had experienced were examined. Comparisons were then drawn between those in the very low or low literacy and very low numeracy groups and their counterparts without basic skills problems in four areas of life: Education and Employment, Training and Occupational Achievement, Family Life, Health and Public Participation.

Extent of the Difficulties

- Excluding writing, assessments showed that in literacy 6% had very low skills and 13% low skills. In numeracy 19% of men and 27% of women had very low skills.

- Based on self report, spelling was the most widely reported difficulty. Extracting specific information from a passage of text proved to be the most demanding literacy task; 1 in 5 had difficulties with such tasks. Area measurement and service charge calculations were the most difficult numeracy tasks - 3 in 4 women and 2 in 3 men could not do these tasks.

Education and Employment

▶ The educational careers of people in the lowest literacy and numeracy groups were marked by an early exit from school at 16, and non-attainment of any formal qualification.

▶ The employment careers of men were subsequently characterised by periods of unemployment, and in the case of women, by early exit from the labour market usually to look after their families.

▶ Men and women with poor skills tended to be concentrated in the unskilled and manual areas of the labour market.

Training and Occupational Achievement

▶ Men and women with poor basic skills had restricted opportunities to advance their careers: far fewer had experience of work-based training, courses leading to qualifications, or had ever been promoted.

▶ Fewer reported having good work-related skills especially in key areas of modern employment such as computing.

▶ Many more earned a low weekly wage: half the women with low literacy skills earned less than, £150 per week compared with two fifths of women with good literacy skills.

Family Life

▶ Among cohort members who left school at 16, those with poor basic skills had more children at an earlier age.

▶ There was a tendency for more of both partners in families identified with poor basic skills to be out of work: 1 in 10 of those with very low literacy skills, and 1 in 12 with low skills compared with 2 in 100 of those with good literacy skills.

▶ Housing Association or Council accommodation was rented by 1 in 3 with very low literacy, 1 in 4 with very low numeracy, 1 in 5 with low literacy skills; just 1 in 20 with good literacy skills were living in rented housing.

Health and Public Participation

▶ Symptoms of poor physical and mental health were reported to a greater degree: 36% of women with very low literacy, 16% with low literacy, 18% with very low numeracy and 12% with low numeracy had symptoms of depression as compared with 7% of those with good literacy and 5% with good numeracy skills .

▶ The depressed state of people with very low literacy or very low numeracy was reflected further in expressions of dissatisfaction with life, poor self esteem and a lack of trust in people. This was particularly so for men.

▶ Participation in public activities, including politics, was significantly lower among people with poor skills than among their counterparts. Just 1 in 5 women and 1 in 10 men with very low and low literacy or very low numeracy skills had ever been involved in a charity, PTA, etc., as compared with 1 in 2 women and 1 in 3 men with good skills.

▶ The great majority of people do vote in elections, but even this indicator of participation was missing for larger numbers of those with poor basic skills: 1 in 3 men and women with very low literacy and 1 in 4 men with low literacy did note vote in 1987, compared with 1 in 5 overall.

Comparisons with the earlier survey of 21 year olds born in 1970 (BCS70) point to a compounding of difficulties as people with poor basic skills get older. In addition, the greater labour market entry problems of the younger cohort in the late 1980s meant that many more of them never experienced proper employment. This predicts an even greater polarisation between the people with poor basic skills and the others as they proceed through adulthood.

Overall, the picture that emerges from the survey is of the vicious circle of disadvantage and marginalisation associated with basic skills problems. Many people are able to lead satisfying lives despite problems with literacy and numeracy, but the dice is clearly loaded against them, their families and their children in so far as future opportunities are concerned.

The ultimate solution lies in an education system which ensures that every child gains the basic skills during initial education. In the meantime the case is clearly made for a continuing if not expanded effort to rectify at least one of the components of this disadvantage in adulthood through the basic skills route. Remedial action to improve literacy and numeracy will not solve all problems, but it will offer at least one means of access to the training and educational opportunities people with basic skills difficulties need.

CHAPTER 1

Background and Methods

Why Basic Skills ?

The ever increasing pace of technological change is changing people's lives in many ways. The number of jobs available is declining, and to maintain employment large numbers of people are likely to change their occupation several times throughout their lives. In the White Paper *Employment in the 90s*, the Department of Employment noted that the half-life of new technological knowledge is only 2.7 years and that "although seven out of ten of the workforce in the year 2000 are now in jobs, most of them will not be in the same jobs" (ED, 1988). The consequences are greater demand for extended education and training for young people before they enter the labour market, and opportunities for continuing education and re-training throughout their working lives. In domestic and leisure life, labour saving devices, tax forms, and complex regulations place further demands upon the individual's cognitive skills. The transition to adulthood and adult citizenship is becoming increasingly a 'navigation' through institutions in a world of ever-increasing complexity (Evans and Heinz, 1994). The German writer Ulrich Beck (1986) coined the term 'risk society' to underline the uncertainties that now pervade all areas of modern life.

In such a situation education becomes not only the vital means of gaining access to work, but increasingly the means of retaining it. This is not only because education provides qualifications which signal to employers different levels and types of achievement. It also imparts to the individual through the learning process a package of skills which are central to *employability*. Underpinning these are the 'basic' skills of literacy and numeracy. Without them educational attainment is stunted, and the critical skills that are built on top of it, through further education and training, are going to be acquired only with difficulty (Bynner, 1996). The outcome is what is increasingly being described as 'social exclusion' from the modern state: relegation to a position of permanent marginalisation on the periphery of the labour market, accompanied by a disadvantaged home life, and apathy towards all forms of public participation, including voting.

Previous Studies

The Social Statistics Research Unit (SSRU) at City University has carried out a series of studies of basic skills for the Adult Literacy and Basic Skills Unit (ALBSU), as it was then, and more recently, for the Basic Skills Agency (BSA). These have brought to light the disadvantaged circumstances of people with poor basic skills, and have begun to unravel their origins. The findings come from two birth cohort studies for which SSRU is responsible (Ekinsmyth et al, 1994). The first is the National Child Development Study (NCDS) which comprises a sample of over 17,000 people *born in a single week in 1958* and followed up subsequently at age 7, 11, 16, 23, 33 and 37 when a ten percent sample was surveyed. The other study, known as the 1970 British Cohort Study (BCS70), is similar in form, beginning with a sample of over 17,000 people *born in a single week in 1970*. This cohort has been followed up subsequently at age 5, 10, 16, 21 (10% sample), and most recently at 26.

The first report on basic skills was based on the NCDS sample at age 23, when a number of questions were asked to cohort members about difficulties they had experienced with the basic skills of reading, writing and numeracy in their everyday lives (ALBSU, 1987). The next study involving the ten per cent sample of BCS70 cohort members of age 21 targeted basic skills more specifically. The main survey interview questions were concerned with education and the transition to employment. They were followed by a half hour basic skills *assessment*, comprising a number of exercises concerning the use of functional literacy and numeracy. These were designed by consultants, Cambridge Training and Development Agency, specially for the survey to tap the different levels of the ALBSU (now BSA) standards - Wordpower and Numberpower (see Appendix). For Wordpower these comprise Foundation Level and *three* higher levels. For Numberpower there is a Foundation Level and *two* higher levels. The critical distinction for this report is between Foundation

Level signifying only a minimal grasp of the basic skill, and people who were reasonably competent in it. For the former group we go further in identifying, for literacy and numeracy respectively, people whose performance in the assessment was *very poor*, ie. they had barely any literacy or numeracy at all.

The literacy tasks varied from extraction of simple information from posters or the 'yellow pages' of a telephone directory right up to questions about the meaning of a relatively complex piece of text. Numeracy tasks similarly involved everyday operations in shops, various measuring operations of the kind performed at home and extraction of information from graphs and timetables. The tasks were presented to the respondents in a conversational mode so as to be as unthreatening as possible. Although a few people felt unable or unwilling to complete the tasks, the great majority were positive about the assessments, finding them easy to do and interesting in helping them to realise what they were and were not able to do with reading tasks and number work. The cohort members were also asked for a self-assessment of their literacy and number work difficulties, using an expanded version of the same set of questions used in the NCDS survey at age 23. Other questions included a psychological test, the Malaise Inventory, which gives an assessment of the individual's psychological state, particularly with respect to depression.

Two reports were published on the BCS70 survey at 21, the first of which examined the relationships between basic skills difficulties and problems in other areas of life, especially education and employment (Ekinsmyth and Bynner, 1994). The second used the longitudinal data in the study to trace the origins of the adult basic skills problems back to early childhood experiences at home and in education (Bynner and Steedman, 1995).

The survey showed clear signs of what appeared to be the onset of a vicious circle in early childhood, whereby the child's family and the school attended get increasingly out of step. The consequence is a poor grasp of literacy and numeracy skills on the child's part which places a brake on further educational progress and is likely to lead in adult life to a wide range of disadvantages including insecure employment, and early exit from the labour market.

In the NCDS 33 year survey, involving all cohort members, time and cost limitations made it impossible to use the BCS70 objective basic skills assessments. Self-report was used to elicit problems, as in the 23 year survey. Most recently at age 37 a further survey was carried out of a 10% sample of NCDS cohort members, comparable to the BCS70 survey, in which a basic skills assessment was included. A new assessment was used comprising a set of functional literacy and numeracy tasks designed by the National Foundation for Educational Research (NFER). The rest of the survey interview comprised questions about employment and family life, together with the Malaise Inventory and additional questions about the literacy and numeracy ability of cohort members children and general feelings about life.

Aims of the 37-year Survey

The 37 year survey of the NCDS cohort served two main purposes. First it gave us the opportunity to test and replicate some of the striking findings about disadvantages associated with basic skills problems in the BCS70 cohort. Secondly, the BCS70 survey of 21 year olds restricted employment experience largely to those who had left school at the minimum age. At the time of the survey many were still involved in higher education; relatively few had settled down with partners and had children. The 37 year old survey offered the opportunity to examine the effect of basic skills difficulties on employment over a much more extended period of working and family life. Thirty seven is an age when most people have settled into some form of occupation and large numbers will also have got married and had children. Their age puts them at the heart of what we mean by adulthood, exercising the roles and responsibilities of fully independent citizens (Jones and Wallace, 1992). They also confront challenges which are rarer in a younger cohort. Those who have had families will have been involved in helping their own children acquire the basic skills which places added pressure on those whose own grasp of the basic skills is poor.

Assessments

The functional literacy and numeracy tests designed by NFER comprised eight literacy tasks and nine numeracy tasks. Each task consisted of a visual stimulus, such as a page from 'yellow pages', or items to purchase in a shop, and a number of questions about it or exercises to be performed (see Appendix). The tasks were grouped at different levels corresponding to the BSA Word Power and Number Power standards with a reasonable spread of tasks at each level. Each question was coded as correctly answered, incorrectly answered, or not attempted. When a respondent failed to answer three consecutive questions correctly, the assessment was judged to have been completed and no further questions were asked. Three respondents on the literacy assessment and twelve on the numeracy assessment fell into this category. For all the others a score based on aggregating correct answers across all the individual tasks was then calculated separately for literacy and numeracy. The literacy tasks yielded a maximum score of 23; the numeracy tasks a maximum score of 18.

Response

The survey was carried out by the MORI research organisation, who also conducted the BCS70 survey. As in the BCS70 survey, because we were using new assessment tasks and mostly new interviewers, there was extensive piloting to make sure that the assessment exercises all worked and the procedures were clear for administering them. In the event, few difficulties were experienced in carrying out the survey, and interviewers reported that most respondents appeared to have enjoyed participating in it. The response overall was also satisfactory for a survey of this kind. Of the 2144 cohort members originally selected for the survey, 1714 took part in the interviews - ie. a response rate of 79%. Of these, 1711 completed satisfactory literacy assessments and 1702 satisfactory numeracy assessments. The total sample for analysis involving either the literacy or the numeracy scores was therefore 1711.

Comparisons of key characteristics with the 1991 NCDS survey at age 33 allow us to check whether the sample is representative. Table 1.1 shows the percentages who were men, the percentages recording different levels of highest qualification achieved and the percentages who were married and had children. A slightly smaller proportion of men took part in the 37 year survey. There was a small percentage shift towards the married and those with children, and slightly fewer had either *no* qualifications or a degree level qualification. However, the overall picture across the two surveys is remarkably similar. We therefore have confidence that the 37 year sample is representative, with respect to the NCDS cohort at 33.

Table 1.1
Compatibility of NCDS at 33 and 10% sample at 37

Key Indicators	Age 33	Age 37
Gender (% Male)	49.2	46.7
Marital Status (% not married at 33)	20.1	17.5
Parent Status (% no children at 33)	31.1	28.6
Highest Qualification: No qualification at 33	14.7	13.3
Degree level at 33	12.3	11.3
n = 11407		*1714*

In interpreting the findings, however, we also need to be aware that over the whole period of the study from birth, there has inevitably been some drop-out which tends to be concentrated slightly more in the less educated groups. This suggests that the figures we present later for basic skills difficulties are, if anything, conservative. The true extent of the problem we reveal is likely to be greater.

What the Study has Found Out

In interpreting the findings, we make reference to what was found in the earlier BCS70 survey, carried out when the cohort members were 21. These comparisons are useful in pointing to the repetition from one generation to the next of the problems associated with basic skills difficulties.

Because of the more difficult labour market faced by the BCS70 cohort when they left school, one might expect that poor basic skills in the NCDS sample of 37 year olds would have had a less damaging impact upon their lives. We might expect that most would have obtained reasonably secure employment and settled down in family life. The findings from the survey give little support for such a prediction. There were strong indications that the consequences of poor literacy and numeracy, inherited from bad education, compounded the problems that the NCDS cohort members faced as they moved through adulthood.

The gap between the literate and the barely literate, and the numerate and the barely numerate, got larger on a number of key indicators. Those with literacy and numeracy problems had much more patchy careers; many more were unemployed at the time of the survey or out of the labour market engaged in child care. They had married or had children early, had large families, and experienced separation and divorce to a much larger extent. They reported symptoms of physical and mental health problems to a greater degree. Their participation in public activities, including politics, was significantly lower than that of their counterparts.

Overall, the picture that emerges from the survey is that the vicious circle of disadvantage and marginalisation associated with basic skills problems continues through adult life. A lack of basic skills during adulthood is characterised by poor job opportunities, lack of further education and training, and a tendency towards a stressful personal and family life. We conclude that although much of the focus in basic skills work has shifted rightly to work with children in schools, the needs of adults in this area are as pressing as ever.

The Report

The report is organised to address each of the key questions of the study. First we use the literacy and numeracy assessment scores to identify people with severe functional difficulties, and then provide details of what kind of difficulties these were (Chapter 2) . The bulk of the report then examines how people with poor literacy and numeracy fared in comparison with their counterparts without basic skills problems in four areas of life: [Education and Employment (Chapter 3), Training and Occupational Achievement (Chapter 4), Family Life (Chapter 5), Health and Participation in Public Life (Chapter 6)]. The report ends with some general conclusions concerning the relationship between basic skills problems and social exclusion, and what needs to be done to overcome this.

We attempt to identify the effects of basic skills problems over and above those associated with leaving school at 16. To do this, two types of analysis were routinely carried out - one for the total sample, and one restricted to cohort members who left school at the minimum age of 16. Finally, to bring the figures to life, in Appendix 4, thumbnail sketches are supplied of the lives of selected sample members with basic skills difficulties.

CHAPTER 2

Defining Poor Literacy and Numeracy

Before we can begin to examine the relationship of poor numeracy and literacy to difficulties in other areas of life, we need to identify those cohort members who performed in the literacy and numeracy assessments at different levels, especially those whose performance was poor. In this chapter we examine the distribution of literacy and numeracy difficulties as revealed by the assessments. We also use the additional information that cohort members provided about their own difficulties, to identify the areas where remediation is most needed.

Who has poor basic skills?

As noted in Chapter 1, the eight literacy tasks and nine numeracy tasks that cohort members completed contained twenty-three and eighteen questions respectively. For those who completed the assessment satisfactorily, a score of one was allocated to each correct answer. Aggregate literacy and numeracy scores were then produced by summing the individual scores within a range of 0-23 for literacy and 0-18 for numeracy. Figures 2.1a and 2.1b show the percentages of cohort members obtaining each score within these ranges.

It is important to note that the literacy tasks assessed reading, but not writing. Evidence from other surveys conducted by the Basic Skills Agency shows that a higher proportion of the population has difficulty with spelling and writing than with reading. The scores reported in this study therefore understate the overall number of adults who have problems with literacy, when that includes writing as well as reading.

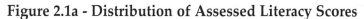

Figure 2.1a - Distribution of Assessed Literacy Scores

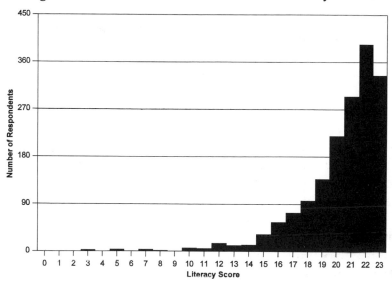

Figure 2.1b - Distribution of Assessed Numeracy Scores

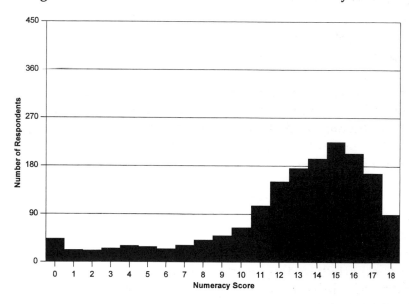

The literacy scores show that people had problems, predominantly, with the harder tasks. The numeracy scores were more evenly distributed and people were failing to master many of the numeracy tasks. Again for ease of interpretation and comparability with BCS70 the literacy and numeracy scores were re-scaled to fall within a range of ten. Table 2.1 shows the *arithmetic means* (averages) of the re-scaled scores for male and female cohort members separately, and for the total sample on literacy and numeracy. The *standard deviations* ('sd') - a measure of variability of the scores about the mean scores - are also shown. The larger the standard deviation the more spread out the scores were, i.e., there were more high *and* more low scores.

Table 2.1
Mean Scores obtained in Literacy and Numeracy Assessments

	Literacy			**Numeracy**		
	Mean	sd**	N	Mean	sd**	N
All	8.8	1.2	1711*	6.9	2.4	1702
Men	8.9	1.1	799	7.3	2.3	799
Women	8.7	1.3	912	6.6	2.5	903
Max Score	10			10		

* 3 cohort members did not complete any literacy tasks; 12 cohort members did not complete any numeracy tasks.
** sd =standard deviation

The cohort members had a lower mean score on the numeracy assessment than the literacy assessment, and also showed much more variability in their numeracy scores than in their literacy scores as indicated by the standard deviations (sd). The standard deviations also enable us to establish statistical confidence intervals for the scores, i.e. the interval in which we could be confident at odds of 19 to 1 (against being wrong) that the score for the whole population falls. The confidence interval for the literacy assessment is 8.7 to 8.9 and for the numeracy assessment it is 6.8 to 7.0. Although the mean literacy score was much the same for men and women, for numeracy the mean score was significantly lower for women than for men, showing again women's greater overall difficulty with the numeracy tasks.

To simplify the presentation of findings and pinpoint more precisely the poorest literacy and numeracy, the raw scores were next grouped into four ability categories 'very low', 'low', 'average' and 'good'. The cut-off points for these groups reflected natural breaks in the distributions of scores and also points where there were marked differences in the characteristics of the people in the groups. Table 2.2a gives the percentages of male and female cohort members falling into these ability groups for both literacy and numeracy. The ranges of scores defining each group are also shown. Table 2.2b gives the mean and standard deviations of the (re-scaled) scores in each of these groups.

Table 2.2a
Distribution of Men and Women by Assessed
Literacy and Numeracy Ability

Literacy Ability					
Raw Scores	**V. Low** (0-15)	**Low** (16-18)	**Average** (19-21)	**Good** (22-23)	*N*
All(%)	6	13	38	43	*1711*
Men(%)	5	11	37	47	*799*
Women(%)	7	16	39	39	*912*
Numeracy Ability					
Raw Scores	**V. Low** (1-10)	**Low** (11-13)	**Average** (14-15)	**Good** (22-23)	*N*
All(%)	23	25	25	27	*1702*
Men(%)	19	23	24	34	*799*
Women(%)	27	28	25	21	*903*

Table 2.2b
Mean Scores Attained in Literacy Test by
Literacy Ability & Numeracy Test by Numeracy Ability

<u>Literacy Ability</u>

	Very Low Mean	sd	Low Mean	sd	Average Mean	sd	Good Mean	sd
Men	5.6	1.1	7.5	0.34	8.8	0.34	9.8	0.22
n =	(40)		(85)		(299)		(375)	
Women	5.1	1.5	7.4	0.35	8.8	0.34	9.8	0.22
n =	(62)		(142)		(354)		(354)	

<u>Numeracy Ability</u>

	Very Low Mean	sd	Low Mean	sd	Average Mean	sd	Good Mean	sd
Men	3.3	1.9	6.8	0.45	8.1	0.28	9.3	0.42
n =	(148)		(184)		(195)		(272)	
Women	3.1	1.9	6.7	0.43	8.1	0.28	9.3	0.42
n =	(241)		(249)		(224)		(189)	

These two tables show that 6% of the population had very low literacy scores (as indicated by the low mean values). The proportion with very low numeracy scores was (23%). In the case of numeracy, substantially more women fell into this 'very low' category than men; 27% of women compared with 19% of men. The figures also give us some indication of performance in relation to the BSA standards. Thus people in the *very low* groups were generally below the Wordpower and Numberpower Foundation Levels in the skills they had acquired and those in the *low* groups were at, or barely scraping above, Foundation Level. In subsequent analyses we focus particularly on the ways in which cohort members in the *very low* and *low* literacy and *very low* numeracy groups differed from the others in terms of other characteristics. But first we examine the cohort members' performance on the individual tasks.

Table 2.3
% Men and Women who answered Literacy Questions <u>incorrectly</u>

QUESTIONS	All %	Men %	Women %
FOUNDATION LEVEL			
1. A newspaper advert for a Concert...			
a. Where was the concert being held ?	6	6	6
b. Who will be playing the concert ?	<1	<1	<1
2. A letter was given to read...			
a. What does Jo want Pat to do for her ?	4	4	4
b. Why does she ask Pat to do shopping ?	3	4	3
c. What time does Jo expect to return ?	2	2	2
3. Instructions for replacing a battery...			
a. Where is the battery compartment found ?	2	1	2
b. Which of the old batteries should be removed first ?	9	4	13
c. Which of the three batteries should be inserted first ?	10	6	13
LEVEL 1			
1. Reading a newspaper extract about a cat (Whisky)...			
a. What was Whisky's condition ?	32	33	30
b. How did she survive without food ?	8	7	8
c. Where is Whisky now ?	4	5	4
2. Consulting Yellow Pages...			
a. From the index pages, which page are details of plumbers on ?	22	21	24
b. What is the telephone number of a Plumber in Chiswick ?	5	5	6
LEVEL 2			
1. Reading a Conservation Article			
a. How many types of grass are there in the world ?	8	6	10
b. Names of 3 types of cereal ?	7	8	7
c. Which cereal grows well in poor, sandy soil ?	17	15	19
d. How is flour made from wheat ?	15	16	14
2. Reading Information about a Town...			
a. In which year during 1965-1982, was the most new factory space made available?	21	17	24
b. What % of people work in the Town Centre ?	20	17	24
c.. How do we know that the pedestrian walkways are successful ?	15	14	15
LEVEL 3			
1. 'True' or 'False' to an article on Households and Families			
a. Between 1971 - 1991, the number of divorces more than trebled.	28	20	35
b. Since 1971 there was a decrease in people who live alone.	20	18	22
c. In 1991, over 17% of families with children were headed by a lone mother.	13	13	13
n= . 1711		*799*	*912*

What are the difficulties?

The literacy and numeracy assessment provided examples of the kinds of tasks men and women have to perform in their everyday lives. The self-reported skills problems show where they themselves identified their difficulties.

Literacy Tasks

Table 2.3 compares male and female failure rates and the overall failure rate for each of the tasks grouped in accordance with the Wordpower standards. Broadly, with some exceptions, the failure rates corresponded to the levels of difficulty defined by the BSA standards, showing marked discrepancies by literacy ability, especially for tasks at the highest Wordpower levels. The failure rates were comparable for men and women except for one Foundation Level task concerning instructions for changing the battery in a video recorder (question FL.3b), which defeated more women than men (13% in comparison with 4%). Also one third of women could not interpret graphical information about households and families (question L3.1a) compared with one fifth of men.

As we would expect, the failure rates differed across the four literacy groups. Figure 2.2 shows the tasks for which the difference between the groups was largest (Table A1, Appendix, shows this comparison for all of the tasks for men and women separately).

Four fifths of men and women in the *very low* literacy group could not interpret the graphical information about divorce rates; or correctly extract statistical information about factory space from an article about a town (question L2.2a); and over two thirds could not extract information about plumbers from "Yellow Pages" (question L1.2a). This compared with failure rates of less than one fifth for each of these questions for the good skills group. There were hardly any differences in the rates for men and women in the average and good literacy groups but in the low literacy groups much more differentiation between the sexes was again apparent (Table A1, Appendix). For example: 42% of men compared with 27% of women could not say how flour was made from wheat; 58% of women compared with 37% of men could not extract statistical information from an article about a town.

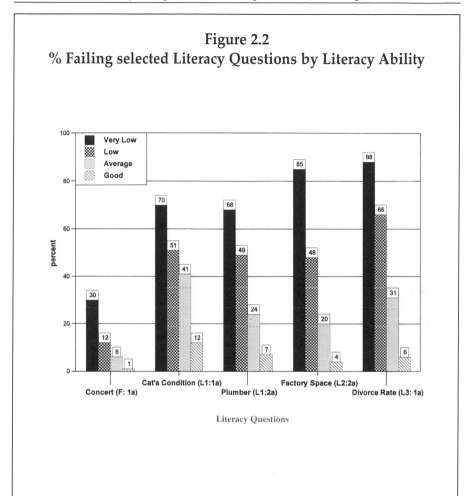

Figure 2.2
% Failing selected Literacy Questions by Literacy Ability

Numeracy Tasks

Table 2.4 compares male and female failure rates and the overall failure rate for each of the tasks grouped in accordance with the Numberpower standards. As for literacy, the failure rates corresponded broadly to the levels of difficulty defined by the BSA standards.

In contrast to their performance on the literacy tasks, women showed consistently higher failure rates for all the numeracy tasks.

Table 2.4
% Men and Women who answered Numeracy Tasks <u>incorrectly</u>

QUESTIONS	All %	Men %	Women %
FOUNDATION LEVEL			
1.Doing Shopping for a neighbour...			
a. How much change should you give after shopping ?	26	25	28
2. Planning a route for a job interview...			
a..Which train should you catch to arrive at the company in time ?	21	22	20
b. What time will you arrive at the company ?	34	33	35
3. Amount of Floor Space in a room...			
a. Calculate the area of a room in square feet.	36	26	46
LEVEL 1			
1. Ordering a Pizza with friends...			
a. What is the total cost ?	11	10	13
b. How much does each person have to pay ?	17	16	19
2. Digging a garden pond...			
a. What is the area of pond liner required ?	65	56	73
3. Information on Council Spending from a Chart...			
a. What was the 1993 Education spending to the nearest £1 million ?	28	24	32
b. What was the 1994 Fire department spending to nearest million ?	27	21	32
c. Which department spent nearly £6 million in 1994 ?	8	5	10
LEVEL 2			
1. Two families go to a restaurant...			
a. What is the total bill, including 12½% service charge ?	69	65	73
2. Details of credit schemes to buy furniture on...			
a. Which is the cheapest way of paying monthly ?	16	14	18
b. Which is the cheapest way of paying overall ?	18	16	20
c. And by how much cheaper is it overall ?	39	34	43
3. How much do people spend on food, fuel, shelter...			
a. What % of income spent on above if earn £10,000 per year ?	14	12	16
b. What % of income does someone in USA spend if they earn £30,000 per year?	18	16	22
c. What relationship between earnings and cost of living does the graph show from 1993 ?	55	53	58
d. What is the % difference between the rise in earnings and the rise in cost of living in 1994?	44	37	50
n=	1702	799	903

The biggest differences between men and women were for tasks concerned with the calculation of areas (FL.3a and L1.2a) and working with percentages (L2.1a). For example, 46% of women compared with 26% of men could not work out the area of a room in square feet (FL.3.a) and 73% of women compared with 65% of men could not work out the cost of a 12.5% service charge in a restaurant (L2.1a).

There were very marked discrepancies in the failure rates between the different numeracy ability groups, especially for tasks at the highest Numberpower levels. Although some unexpected failures were recorded for Foundation Level tasks by men and women with average/good numeracy skills. Figure 2.3 shows some examples of tasks for which the differences were largest. (The figures for all the tasks are given in Table A2, Appendix). Working out the time of arrival at a destination (FL.2b) was beyond three quarters of men and women in the very low numeracy group compared with one twentieth of the good skills group. Over four fifths of the very low numeracy group could not do the tasks concerning information on Council spending from a chart (L1.3a), or the details of a credit scheme (L2.2c) compared with 1% and 6% respectively of the good skills group. The task which discriminated between the groups most was working out the area of a complex shape in the form of a garden pond liner (L1.2a). This was beyond 99% of those with very low numeracy skills, whereas only a quarter of those with good skills could not do it.

Self-Reported Difficulties

The objective assessments give the best indication of skills acquired, but how individuals react to their difficulties may be as much to do with whether they perceive themselves to have a problem as whether they actually have one. Many people who, in terms of basic skill standards, are high up the scale may nevertheless worry about skills deficiencies because the occupations they are in demand high levels of skill. For example those in journalism will be conscious of the need for literacy skills. Despite these difficulties in interpreting self-reports of basic skills problems, the earlier work showed the majority of people who said they had problems also obtained low scores on the assessments (Ekinsmyth and Bynner, 1994). However,

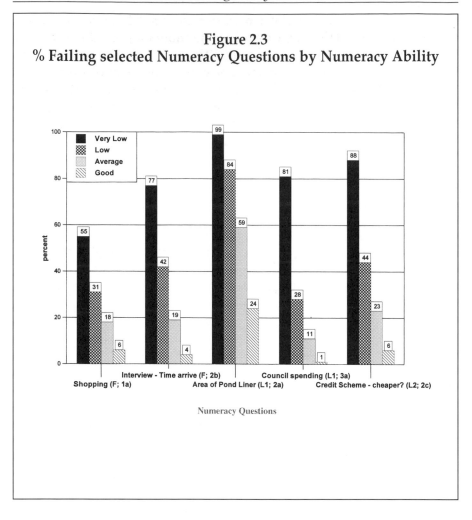

Figure 2.3
% Failing selected Numeracy Questions by Numeracy Ability

perhaps because of the low priority attached to numeracy skills in most areas of employment, many people with low numeracy scores did not acknowledge that they had difficulty with numberwork. The main value of self-reports is to point to the kinds of literacy and numeracy tasks that people perceive to be most difficult. We can also see how these differ between surveys.

Table 2.5 compares the self-reported difficulties by NCDS cohort members age 37 with those reported by the whole NCDS sample at age 23, and the BCS70 cohort members at age 21. In these earlier surveys, between 11% - 13% of cohort members reported difficulties with either reading, writing/spelling or number work or combinations of them. In the current survey this overall proportion increased slightly to 15% (though this may be because of a slight change in question wording). Overall, at the level of the different kinds of basic skill - reading for example - there was a remarkable consistency from one survey to the next.

Table 2.5
Self-Reported Difficulties in NCDS and BCS70

	NCDS (age 37)			NCDS (age 23)			BCS70 (age 21)		
	All	Men	Women	All	Men	Women	All	Men	Women
Reading	3%	4%	2%	4%	5%	3%	3%	5%	2%
Writing	1%	1%	0%	-	-	-	-	-	-
Spelling	9%	11%	8%	-	-	-	-	-	-
Write & Spell	3%	4%	1%	-	-	-	-	-	-
Write *or* Spell	12%	16%	9%	9%	12%	7%	9%	11%	7%
Numberwork	4%	3%	5%	5%	5%	5%	4%	3%	4%
Any Difficulty	15%	18%	12%	13%	15%	11%	12%	14%	10%
N =	1714	801	913	9757	4725	5032	1632	764	868

The people who performed badly on the literacy and numeracy tests tended to be more aware of literacy and numeracy problems than those who scored well. On the other hand, remarkably high proportions in the low scoring groups appeared either unaware or unable to acknowledge their poor grasp of literacy and numeracy. Thus over three quarters (78%) of women in the low scoring groups did not report any difficulties with literacy or numeracy. In the case of numeracy, the comparable percentages were even higher, 94% of low-scoring women and 85% of low-scoring men did not acknowledge any problem with numeracy.

Literacy difficulties

Cohort members who reported any difficulties with reading, writing or spelling or number work were asked about the specific difficulties they had experienced. The small numbers involved meant that men and women's difficulties could not be examined separately. Figure 2.4 gives the percentages reporting each kind of difficulty.

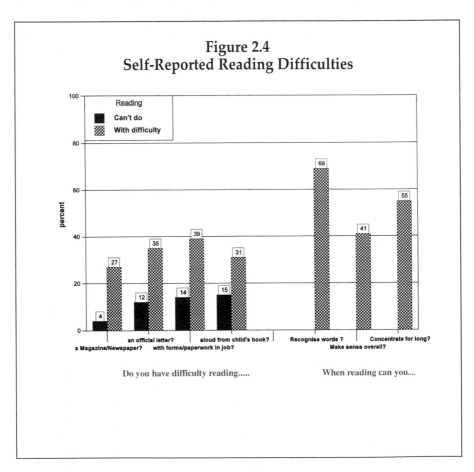

Figure 2.4
Self-Reported Reading Difficulties

Cohort members who said they had difficulties with reading were asked about the tasks that caused them most difficulty. Of those who said they had difficulties, not being able to read a book to a child or to deal with formal paperwork were reported by up to 15%. Around twice this proportion said they could do the tasks but only with difficulty. Of the specific technical tasks involved in reading, recognising words was most frequently reported as being difficult, followed by concentrating for long and, finally, making sense of an overall piece of text.

Writing problems and spelling difficulties were more frequently reported (Figure 2.5). The dominant problem was overwhelmingly spelling. 95% of respondents in the group who said they had difficulty, reported problems with it. The proportions saying they had difficulty with handwriting and expressing themselves in writing were much lower - 18% and 33% respectively.

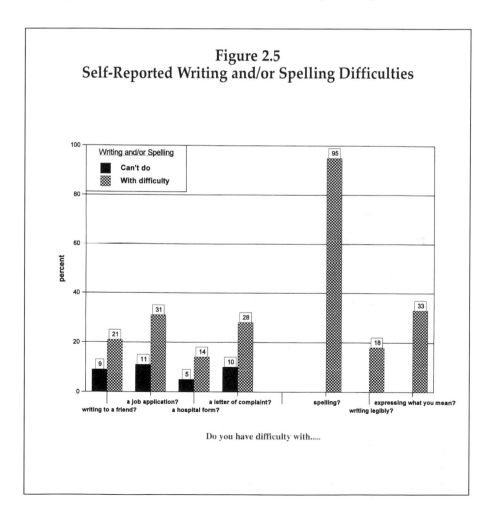

Figure 2.5
Self-Reported Writing and/or Spelling Difficulties

Numberwork difficulties

Those cohort members who said they had difficulties with numberwork were asked in which areas their problems lay. Figure 2.6 shows that three-quarters of men and women who reported numberwork difficulties had problems with the technique of division; over half (57%) reported subtraction to be difficult. 15% reported being unable to manage simple household accounts, and another 8% said they could only manage them with difficulty. As many as 12% of men and women said they had problems in even recognising numbers.

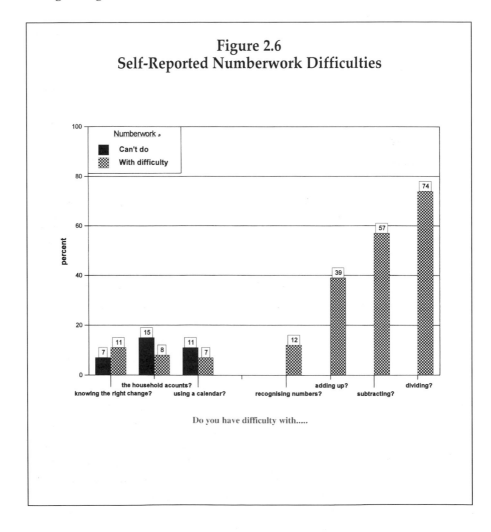

Figure 2.6
Self-Reported Numberwork Difficulties

Courses to help overcome skill difficulties?

Over half of the men and women who reported difficulties with basic skills reported that they had been able to mitigate their specific difficulty. But strategies for doing this varied. Very few had *ever* attended a skills improvement course after they had left school: only 18% of those who reported reading difficulties, 16% of those who reported numberwork difficulties, 13% with writing difficulties and 7% with spelling difficulties. Although still very low, this course attendance was higher than that reported by the younger BCS70 cohort. At age 21, 9% of those who reported reading difficulties, 4% of those who reported writing and/or spelling difficulties and 5% of those who reported numberwork difficulties had been on a skills improvement course.

These figures suggest that as people get older more take some remedial action for their basic skills problem. This underlines the need to continue to target these older age groups for remedial basic skills teaching.

Summary & Conclusions

The NCDS survey of adults at 37 shows that just under one in ten were unable to do most of the reading tasks. Nearly one in five were unable to do most of the numeracy tasks. Women scored consistently lower on numeracy.

Understanding complex text and extracting information from graphs proved to be the most difficult literacy tasks and using measurements to calculate areas and working out percentages the most difficult numeracy tasks, especially for women. Those in the low scoring literacy and numeracy groups compared with those in the average/good scoring groups had exceptional difficulty with these.

The subjective reports of difficulties similarly corresponded to those found previously. Up to one in six people indicated that they had some kind of problem with reading, writing, spelling, or number work. As far as literacy problems were concerned, almost two thirds reporting a problem said they had difficulties with recognising words. With respect to writing and spelling difficulties, spelling was most frequently mentioned, with 95% saying it was a problem for them. For numeracy, of those reporting problems, dividing, subtracting, adding up, and recognising numbers in that order were reported as causing difficulty, with three quarters mentioning dividing. With respect to the use of numbers in everyday life, in shops and at home, doing household accounts came up most frequently as presenting problems: one in five could not do them or could do them only with difficulty.

Finally, although those who reported problems with literacy or numeracy were much more likely than the others to have attended remedial classes to help them, the actual numbers involved were relatively small: 18% of those reporting literacy problems had attended such classes and 16% of those reporting numeracy problems. These figures were over twice those in the comparable BCS70 survey, which suggests that as people get older they do seek help with their problems. However the great majority remain untouched by the learning opportunities available. This suggests considerable scope for targeting much larger numbers of people for literacy and numeracy training.

CHAPTER 3

Education and Employment

Introduction

Basic skills difficulties are implicated in failure at every stage of an educational career. They are fundamental to poor achievement at the earliest stages of primary schooling, and subsequently restrict progress in every area of education that follows it. In the BCS70 survey this was shown by the strong connection between competence in the basic skills and the school qualifications obtained, and following school, those obtained from further education (Ekinsmyth and Bynner, 1994). Young people with poor basic skills appeared to miss out on employment opportunities and frequently found themselves unemployed or on training schemes.

In examining the childhood antecedents of these adult performances (Bynner and Steedman, 1995), we saw evidence of a growing gap between those making normal progress and those falling behind through basic skills problems. Although most parents were enthusiastic about education at the time of their children's entry to primary school, among those with basic skills problems this rapidly dissipated as the home and school became increasingly out of step. As the child fell behind his or her peers, the prospect of catching up became increasingly remote.

Qualifications

The sum total of a person's educational achievements by the age of 37 is indicated by the highest qualification obtained. Cohort members indicated which of a large number of qualifications they had achieved. These were then classified at a number of levels corresponding broadly to the NVQ/GNVQ classification of Level 1 to Level 5. Of particular interest were those cohort members who by the age of 37 had still obtained no formal qualifications.

Highest Qualification at 37

Figure 3.1 shows that moving down through the four literacy and the four numeracy groups (left to right in the diagrams), the proportions *without* a formal qualification (shown by the *black* bars) massively increased. Barely any men and women in the top basic skills groups were *without* formal qualifications by age 37. In sharp contrast, nearly *half* the men and women with very low literacy skills had not achieved any qualification. For those with very low numeracy skills the proportions *without* formal qualifications were generally lower: 31% of men; 23% of women.

These percentages are very similar to those obtained in BCS70. However the percentages gaining some kind of basic qualification was larger for the 37 year olds suggesting that some had been able to get over the hurdle of poor basic skills to obtain qualifications -

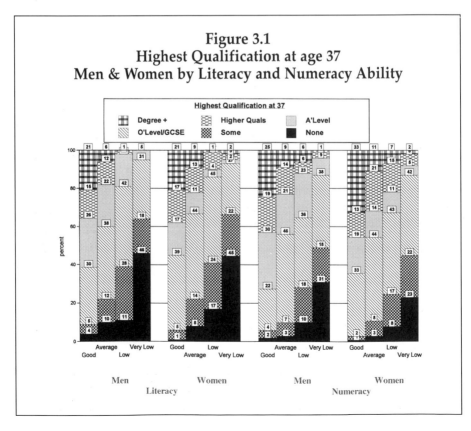

Figure 3.1
Highest Qualification at age 37
Men & Women by Literacy and Numeracy Ability

especially vocational qualifications. Thus by age 37, 31% of men and 27% of women in the very low literacy group had achieved a qualification up to the equivalent of 'O' level, RSA Stage 2 or City and Guilds operative; 5% had reached the equivalent of 'A' level or higher! In BCS70 none of the cohort members had reached this level.

Age of Leaving Full-Time Education

Not surprisingly, poor achievements in education were reflected in early leaving. Table 3.1 shows that around nine tenths of men and three quarters of women with very low or low literacy or very low numeracy skills had left full-time education at the minimum age, 16. No men or women with *very low literacy* scores, or men with *low literacy* scores, had been involved in education post-18. In contrast, one-quarter of men and women with *good literacy* skills and one-third of men and women with *good numeracy* skills had remained in full-time education post-18.

Table 3.1
Age Men and Women Left Full-Time Education
by Literacy and Numeracy Ability

	Literacy				Numeracy			
	V. Low	Low	Average	Good	V. Low	Low	Average	Good
	%	%	%	%	%	%	%	%
Men								
Age 16	83	91	72	47	91	80	66	35
Post 16	17	9	21	26	7	17	24	32
Post 18	-	-	7	27	2	3	10	33
n=	(30)	(70)	(244)	304)	(114)	(148)	(159)	(228)
Women								
Age 16	80	74	55	38	73	57	45	29
Post 16	20	23	34	37	23	34	39	38
Post 18	-	3	11	25	4	9	16	33
n=	(41)	(108)	(307)	(310)	(188)	(213)	(194)	(167)

Employment and Unemployment

Full time employment is the experience of the great majority of men. Women's relationship to the labour market is more complex, with periods of withdrawal from it into part-time employment, unemployment and home-care, often connected with having and caring for children (Bynner, Morphy and Parsons, 1996). In BCS70, even at the relatively young age of 21, in response to labour market difficulties, one third of females with poor literacy defined themselves as 'at home'. The same proportion of male respondents with poor literacy defined themselves as ' unemployed'.

Employment Status at 37

In the NCDS survey strong relationships between basic skill difficulties and employment status were again apparent. Those cohort members in the lowest literacy and numeracy skills groups were again least likely to be in employment. Interestingly too, many men who were not employed at the time of the survey, designated themselves as *sick* rather than unemployed. The concentration of this group in the very low literacy and numeracy groups, suggested that the sickness could possibly be masking unemployment[1]. Twenty three per cent of men in the very low literacy group and 19% of those in the very low numeracy group said they were unemployed or sick compared with 4% and 3% respectively in the good literacy and numeracy skills group.

Women's employment showed the greater complexities of their labour market participation. Thus in the very low literacy group 26% were engaged in home care, 31% were in full-time employment and 34% in part-time employment. In the good literacy group the figures were 14% home care, 43% full-time employment and 39% part-time employment.

---

[1]'Sickness' is defined as a *temporary* or *permanent* state - an absence of at least 6 months on a continuous basis from the labour market. 44 people were permanently sick. This group included only 5 men and 3 women who had never worked on a full-time basis. All others had a self-reported sickness which had taken them out of the labour market at some stage in their employment careers. Disability premiums associated with sickness benefit/ income support give a higher financial return than if claiming unemployment benefit/income support. Self esteem could also be somewhat protected by claiming sickness benefit/income support. By being officially told you are 'unfit to work', a reason for not being employed had now been provided.

Employment history

To understand the role of basic skills in labour market participation it is useful to review the whole employment record up to 37. Figures 3.2a and 3.2b[2] show the percentages of men in each of the four literacy and numeracy groups who were working full-time in each year from age 17 to 37. Men assessed with very low or low skills had entered the labour market at an earlier age, hence their higher level of employment initially. But by the early to mid 1980s - a time when any involvement in higher education had all but ceased and the sharp economic recession of that time was in full force - a much higher proportion of men with average or good skills were in full-time jobs. At age 21, approximately 90% of men with very low, low, or average skills were in full-time work (a proportion of men with good skills remained in full-time education). Two years later at age 23, the proportion with very low skills in full-time employment had dropped to almost 80%. In contrast, levels of employment among those with better skills had changed very little. Over time, those with very low and low literacy skills were increasingly less likely to be in full time employment than those with more skills. So, for example, from age 31, 75% of men with very low literacy skills were in full-time work, compared with over 90% of men with good literacy skills.

It was the group of men with *very low* literacy skills who had felt the brunt of the recession most. The problems they had in retaining employment then appeared to stay with them at much the same level right through to their thirties. With respect to numeracy, although much the same employment picture was apparent, it was only men in the *very low* numeracy group that were marked out particularly as having difficulty in maintaining employment.

---

[2] Employment status can differ within an individual year. The employment status attributed to an individual was decided by the highest number of months spent in one employment category during any one year (ie. if 3 months were spent unemployed and 9 months full-time employed, a full-time employment status was allocated. If an equal number of months had been spent unemployed or in full-time work, a full-time employment status was given).

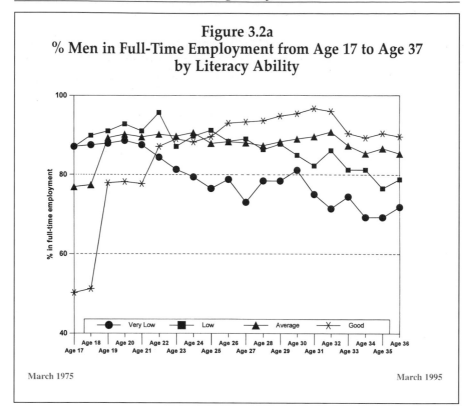

Figure 3.2a
% Men in Full-Time Employment from Age 17 to Age 37
by Literacy Ability

Figure 3.3a and Figure 3.3b give the comparable picture for women. Because of the relatively small number of women who had very low literacy skills and worked full-time, for the purposes of this analysis, the very low and low literacy skill groups were combined. The graphs show the characteristic patterns of women's employment, with increasing numbers leaving full-time employment as age increased and child rearing took over. But as for the men, movement out of full-time employment, and especially its timing, was sharply differentiated across the basic skills groups. Women with very low or low literacy or very low numeracy were the first to enter full-time employment, and the first to leave it. In every year from age 22 they consistently had the lowest proportions working on a full-time basis; between age 29 to 36 just one in three of women with very low or low literacy or very low numeracy skills worked full-time. Over the same seven year period, at least half of the women with good numeracy

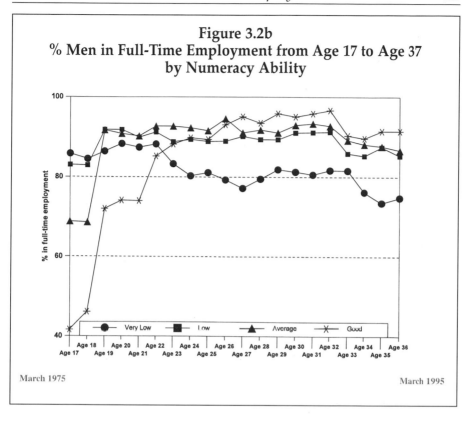

Figure 3.2b
% Men in Full-Time Employment from Age 17 to Age 37 by Numeracy Ability

skills and two fifths of the women with good literacy skills continued in full-time employment.

In contrast with men, the effects of the economic recession at the beginning of the 1980s were not apparent. It has been noted in other studies that somewhat against expectation, women's employment survived the new technology revolution at that time better than men's (Ashton and Maguire, 1986). In general, it is women who leave full-time employment because of child-care or family responsibilities, moving to part-time employment or to becoming 'economically inactive' in the home (Bynner, Morphy and Parsons, 1996). Barely any women in this cohort ever defined themselves as *unemployed*. Displacement from full-time employment because of a contracting labour market is therefore much more difficult to determine for women than it is for men.

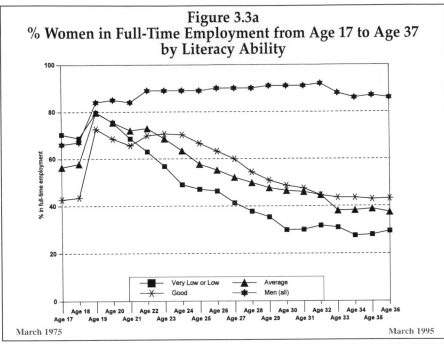

Figure 3.3a
% Women in Full-Time Employment from Age 17 to Age 37
by Literacy Ability

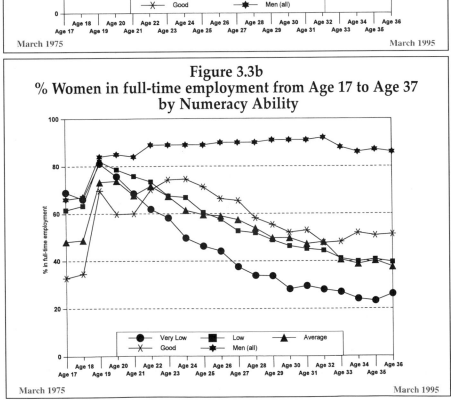

Figure 3.3b
% Women in full-time employment from Age 17 to Age 37
by Numeracy Ability

Labour market experience is tied up at the beginning of a career with the length of involvement in full-time education (men and women) and later on with part-time employment and child care (mostly women). A final perspective on the role of basic skills and the employment of men and women, holds these components constant by concentrating on those cohort members who had left full-time education at 16: ie. the group who potentially had all been exposed to the labour market for the same amount of time (Tables 3.2a & 3.2b).

Table 3.2a
Number of Years Spent in Full-Time Employment between Age 16 - 37:
Men who left Full-Time education at age 16 by Literacy & Numeracy Ability

	None	1-4	5-9	10-14	15-19	20+	Mean	sd	N
Total Years Spent in Full-Time Employment...									
Literacy Ability									
Very Low	4%	12%	8%	12%	12%	**52%**	15.4yrs	7.0	25
Low	5%	3%	8%	16%	14%	**55%**	16.2yrs	6.6	64
Average	1%	6%	3%	6%	23%	**61%**	17.9yrs	5.2	175
Good	-	3%	4%	3%	22%	**69%**	18.9yrs	4.0	142
Numeracy Ability									
Very Low	3%	10%	6%	13%	20%	**46%**	15.5yrs	6.7	104
Low	3%	5%	3%	4%	17%	**68%**	18.1yrs	5.5	118
Average	-	1%	5%	4%	24%	**67%**	18.9yrs	3.7	105
Good	-	3%	1%	6%	15%	**69%**	19.0yrs	3.6	80

Table 3.2b
Number of Years Spent in Full-Time Employment between Age 16 - 37:
Women who left Full-Time education at age 16 by Literacy & Numeracy Ability

	None	1-4	5-9	10-14	15-19	**20+**	Mean	*sd*	N
Total Years Spent in Full-Time Employment...									
Literacy Ability									
Very Low	**18%**	27%	27%	6%	9%	**12%**	7.5yrs	6.8	33
Low	**4%**	20%	35%	24%	9%	**9%**	9.0yrs	6.0	80
Average	**5%**	14%	32%	25%	15%	**10%**	10.2yrs	5.9	168
Good	**3%**	14%	26%	24%	18%	**16%**	11.4yrs	6.1	117
Numeracy Ability									
Very Low	**8%**	23%	22%	21%	10%	**7%**	8.4yrs	5.9	138
Low	**4%**	12%	34%	22%	16%	**12%**	10.7yrs	6.0	121
Average	**5%**	14%	29%	25%	15%	**13%**	10.6yrs	6.2	87
Good	-	13%	19%	25%	21%	**23%**	12.8yrs	5.9	48

The differences between men and women's labour market participation and the effects of basic skills difficulties are strikingly shown by the amount of employment they had notched up by age 37. Men and women who had left school at 16 could have accumulated up to 21 years of full-time employment. Whilst 46% of men in the very low numeracy group had worked full-time for 20+ years, 69% of those with good skills had done so. The average number of years worked for those with very low literacy skills was 15.4 years. For those with good skills it was 18.9 years.

For women the average number of years in full-time employment was quite different. For those women in the very low literacy group the average accumulated full-time employment experience was only 7.5 years compared with 15.4 years for men in the same group. At the higher skills levels there was slightly more convergence, but even those women with very good numeracy skills had accumulated on average only 12.8 years employment experience compared with 19.0 years for the comparable group of men.

These figures also give a more precise picture of the move by women into part-time work at some period of their working lives. Thus the highest percentages for women in all groups were recorded for those who had spent 5-9 years in full-time employment. For men the highest percentages were for 20 or more years. But again these experiences were not spread evenly across the sample. For women in the very low basic skills groups less than four years in employment was far more common than it was for those whose skills were 'average' or 'good'.

So now we can see in sharper profile the effect of basic skills and gender on labour market participation, this time among those with maximum opportunities for it. For people with poor basic skills access to employment is drastically reduced, with women apparently being exceptionally disadvantaged.

Occupation

By 37 we might expect most people's occupational careers to have stabilised. The relatively small sample size restricts the amount of detail about occupation that we are able to bring to light, but the broad occupational profiles can be identified. Because of the low numbers we have combined the very low and low literacy categories. We use the 9 major occupational groups of the Registrar General's Standard Occupational Classification (1991). As shown over the page, occupations concentrated into six groups for men (85% of all men) and a largely different set of six groups for women (85% of all women).

Men
- Managers & Administrators
- Professionals
- Associated Professionals
- Craft & Related
- Plant & Machine Operators
- Other (a myriad of unskilled occupations ie. general labourer, farm-hand, etc).

Women
- Professionals
- Associated Professionals
- Clerical & Secretarial
- Personal/Service
- Sales
- Other.

Again, we examine the occupations of those cohort members who had left full-time education at age 16, so as to compare those with similar exposure to the labour market. Figures 3.4a and 3.4b show respectively for men, the percentages of each literacy and numeracy group falling into each of the six listed occupational categories.

It is clear that men with poor basic skills were overwhelmingly engaged in manual work. With respect to specific occupations, 30% of men with very low numeracy were *Plant & Machine Operatives,* twice the proportion of men in other ability groups. More men with very poor basic skills were also in *Other* occupations. In contrast, men with good numeracy skills were *five times* as likely to be *Managers & Administrators,* or to be a *Professional* or *Associated Professional* in comparison with men in the very low numeracy group. Men with good literacy skills were *twice* as likely to be a *Manager or Administrator,* and three times as likely to be involved in the *Professional* occupations, in comparison with men who had very low or low literacy skills. This suggests that a high premium is placed on numeracy at this level of men's work. No more than *one in ten* men in the lowest numeracy group held management or professional occupations. It was somewhat surprising though to find *any* men with very poor basic skills in this category. This points to a skills deficiency which many men in such occupations would probably be pleased to get rid of.

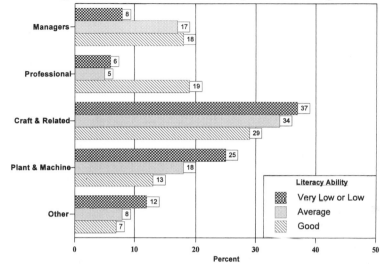

Figure 3.4a
Occupation at 37 for Men who left Full-time Education at 16
% from the total sample in each literacy group
falling into 6 most common occupational categories

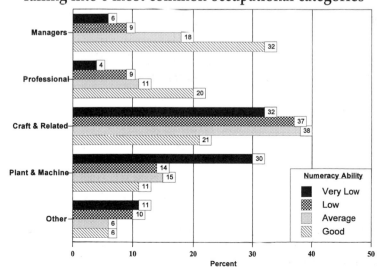

Figure 3.4b
Occupation at 37 for Men who left Full-time Education at 16
% from the total sample in each numeracy group
falling into 6 most common occupational categories

Because of the significance of part-time employment at different stages in many women's working lives, the very clear association between occupations and basic skills was not quite as clear for women as it was for men. For example, many women re-entering the labour market part-time after having children, 'trade down' their occupation by choice or necessity. They take jobs below the level that their qualifications and experience could command (Joshi and Hinde, 1993). Other women of course with poor qualifications have no option but to take the same job because there is nothing else that they are qualified for.

Figures 3.5a and 3.5b give the percentages of women in each of the basic skills groups, working in the different occupational areas. The data points to the attraction of women to non-manual jobs; *Clerical and Secretarial* was by far the biggest occupational category.

The figures also point to a tendency for those with poor basic skills to be pushed into the less skilled kinds of manual occupation either

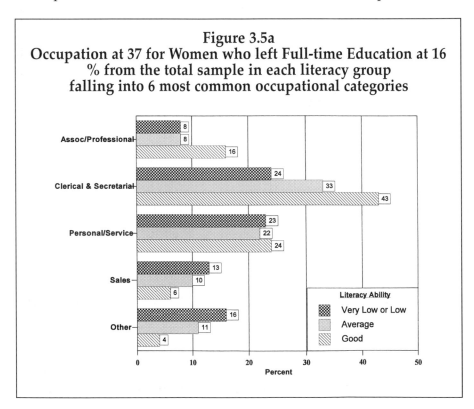

Figure 3.5a
Occupation at 37 for Women who left Full-time Education at 16
% from the total sample in each literacy group
falling into 6 most common occupational categories

in the *Personal/Services* category, which encompasses care-assistants, cleaners, hair-dressers, etc, or especially into the 'rag-bag' *Other* category comprising such jobs as packing and factory work. As for men, numeracy also appeared to have a high premium attached to it for accessing the top jobs. Women with good numeracy skills were *three times* as likely to be employed as *Professionals* or *Associated Professionals* compared with women with low numeracy skills.

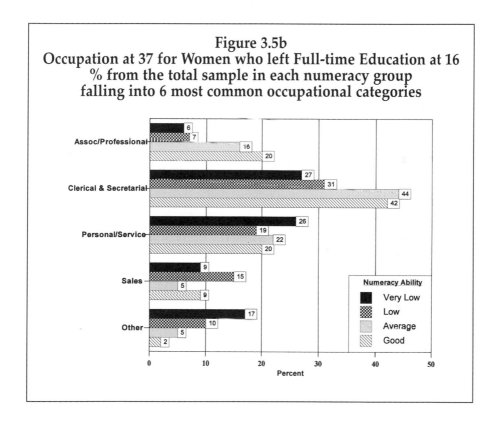

Figure 3.5b
Occupation at 37 for Women who left Full-time Education at 16
% from the total sample in each numeracy group
falling into 6 most common occupational categories

Summary & Conclusions

The data shows disparities in employment opportunities between people with poor literacy or poor numeracy and the others, which get worse as people get older.

The first sign of difficulty comes with the overall highest level of qualification reached, where substantial proportions of people in the lowest literacy and numeracy groups had not achieved any qualifications at all. Their educational careers had been marked by poor performance and leaving school at the minimum statutory age, 16. Their employment careers subsequently were characterised in the case of men, by periods of unemployment, and in the case of women, by early exit from the labour market to look after their families. The occupations entered were again symptomatic of limited opportunities. The men with poor skills tended to be concentrated in plant operative and other forms of unskilled work. Similarly, women with poor skills tended to be in the unskilled and manual areas of the labour market.

This was evident to a greater extent in the NCDS survey than the BCS70 survey, which suggests that labour market and employment problems were compounded as cohort members with poor basic skills got older. These casualised, unskilled areas of the labour market in which they were most frequently to be found, are clearly the place where targeted remedial numeracy and literacy help is needed. On the other hand, another notable finding was that in relatively skilled occupations such as management jobs, substantial minorities also had poor basic skills. There is clearly scope for targeting these kinds of occupations as well.

CHAPTER 4

Training and Occupational Achievement

Training

Training is a critical indicator of the quality of a job. It signifies the investment the employer is prepared to put into the employee and their confidence that it will pay dividends in terms of productivity and progress later on.

There are two types of training of particular relevance to the NCDS cohort. The more successful early school leavers would have had the opportunity to enter an apprenticeship, which was still the dominant form of vocational training in the mid 70s when the cohort members left school. Apprenticeships were, however, targeted heavily at young men entering skilled manual work. Young women tended to go on to a college for an extra year to try and get a secretarial/clerical qualification before seeking a job. Some would take a job and attend college part-time. After this initial training, the amount of training an employee was likely to get depended on the employer and the occupation. Thus professionals such as teachers, nurses and managers would tend to receive this kind of training throughout their careers. Between the ages of 23 and 33 just over one third of men and just under one third of women had actually done a course leading to a qualification. On the other hand, just over half the men and three quarters of the women had *not* done *any* kind of training course lasting three days or more (Bynner and Fogelman, 1993).

As we might expect, both kinds of training were much more common among the groups with good basic skills than in the other groups. Figure 4.1 shows the different kinds of initial training the 16 year old school leavers in the four literacy and numeracy groups had experienced over the period 16-23. Training experiences during these early years were asked about if they had lasted for at least 14 days or

100 hours. Notably, far fewer young women than men had received *any* vocational training (as signified by the black bars in the diagram); virtually none had been on an apprenticeship and those in the lowest literacy or numeracy groups had received the least training of all. Approaching four fifths of the young women in the very low literacy or very low numeracy groups had not received *any* training compared with approximately half of the comparable groups of young men. Even among those young women with 'good' literacy skills, over two fifths had not had any training, whereas for the young men this proportion dropped to below one in nine (11%).

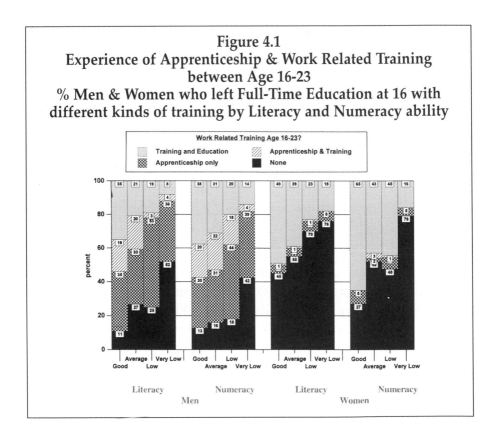

Figure 4.1
Experience of Apprenticeship & Work Related Training between Age 16-23
% Men & Women who left Full-Time Education at 16 with different kinds of training by Literacy and Numeracy ability

The picture changed for work-based training between 23 and 37. Taking the whole sample of cohort members who were in full-time or part-time employment at the time of the interview, much the same proportions of men and women had received *some kind* of training (three days or more between age 23 to 33; at least one day between age 33 to 37). Though men still tended to have been sent on *more* such training courses than had women. Again, however, those in the low basic skills groups were least likely to have received any training. Three fifths of men and women in the lowest literacy group had never been sent on a training course compared with one quarter of women and one fifth of men with good literacy.

The differences for numeracy were in the same direction but generally smaller. When the sample was restricted to those who had left school at 16, much the same picture was apparent.

For the low proportion of cohort members (21% overall) who had taken a course leading to a known qualification between age 33 to 37, further questions were asked about the *kinds* of qualification they were seeking. For those with the poorest skills (just 11% with very low literacy had taken a qualification course), the highest qualification sought was likely to be 'O' Level or NVQ2 equivalent. For those with good skills (30% of women with good literacy skills had taken a qualification-based course) the target was typically a higher education qualification such as a degree or NVQ4 equivalent.

Work-Related Skills

Training courses and qualifications are most often pursued for current employment opportunities or for future career moves. The fast changing labour market calls for new skills to be acquired and old skills to be upgraded, and as we know from earlier work there is a strong relationship between attending training courses and the acquisition of skills (Bynner, 1994). We have seen that men and women with poor literacy or poor numeracy skills have been largely excluded from training throughout their working lives. Without the ever more specialised skills now demanded, how could they expect to compete for jobs on an equal footing?

Respondents were asked in relation to a list of 17 work-related skills drawn up with officials of the (then) Department of Employment whether they thought they were 'good', 'fair', 'poor' or 'did not have' each of the skills. Table 4.1a and Table 4.1b show the percentages of men and women who said they were 'good' at each skill by their literacy and numeracy ability, respectively. A lower proportion of men and women with very low literacy or very low numeracy skills most often perceived themselves to be 'good' at the work-related skill, but the differences varied according to the skill. The skills that men with very low literacy or numeracy skills perceived themselves to lack, (in relation to men in other ability groups), were highly indicative of the jobs they had done and their growing isolation in the labour market. Differences were largest (at least 20%) for: writing, reading plans, computing, teaching, supervision, maths calculations, comprehension, decision making - all skills increasingly demanded by modern employment.

For women, differences between the extremes of those with very low and those with good literacy or numeracy were largest for: writing, reading plans, computing, support/advice, maths calculations, finance, comprehension. Furthermore, only 15% of women with very low literacy skills thought that they had good keyboard skills as compared with 41% of women with good literacy skills. This clearly points to their exclusion from a large area of female employment. Large differences in the proportions of women reporting good teaching or supervision skills were also recorded. In addition, although only one in four of all men and women reported good computing skills, this dropped to just one in twenty men and one in ten women with very low literacy skills.

Good tool use and construction skills were claimed by a higher proportion of men with low literacy or low numeracy skills; for women a higher proportion of those with very low and low literacy or numeracy skills claimed good caring skills. This again reflects the kinds of work in which people with poor basic skills were engaged. Men were able to offer the ability to use tools - the kind of skill they were able to acquire in Britain's largely unregulated building industry: the fact that an equally high proportion of men with very low literacy or numeracy skills [under half] did not even report these skills, adds to their increasing isolation in the changing labour market. Women's experience of caring skills may have been developed looking after children, or through work involving this. Their selling skills were probably acquired through working (often part-time) in shops.

Table 4.1a
% Men & Women Reporting 'Good' Work-Related Skills by Literacy Ability

Specific skill...	MEN				WOMEN			
	Very Low	Low	Average	Good	Very Low	Low	Average	Good
Write clearly	36%	37%	49%	59%	51%	60%	76%	79%
Speak clearly	47%	61%	53%	60%	56%	63%	70%	75%
Use tools correctly	56%	71%	65%	55%	41%	43%	46%	48%
Reading plans	32%	49%	57%	65%	20%	20%	35%	43%
Construction	50%	64%	55%	49%	15%	12%	24%	23%
Type/keyboard	13%	6%	20%	29%	15%	28%	32%	41%
Computing	5%	7%	22%	35%	9%	18%	20%	28%
Providing care	18%	23%	17%	22%	68%	61%	59%	55%
Advice/Support	31%	50%	43%	52%	53%	54%	58%	63%
Teaching	17%	32%	32%	44%	34%	42%	52%	56%
Supervising others	35%	43%	46%	55%	24%	37%	41%	43%
Maths calculations	22%	32%	42%	56%	16%	16%	37%	39%
Selling products	14%	25%	25%	27%	22%	19%	22%	19%
Finance/accounting	22%	21%	25%	34%	10%	16%	31%	29%
Organisation	14%	29%	31%	37%	17%	19%	23%	22%
Comprehension	31%	41%	58%	74%	23%	39%	64%	73%
Decision Making	44%	55%	58%	64%	39%	58%	54%	50%
N =	(37)	(85)	(298)	(372)	(61)	(141)	(354)	(353)

Table 4.1b
%Men & Women Reporting 'Good' Work-Related Skills
by Numeracy Ability

Specific skill...	MEN				WOMEN			
	Very Low	Low	Average	Good	Very Low	Low	Average	Good
Write clearly	37%	47%	48%	65%	61%	76%	74%	83%
Speak clearly	51%	54%	51%	66%	63%	72%	72%	74%
Use tools correctly	58%	68%	63%	55%	45%	43%	48%	49%
Reading plans	36%	56%	62%	70%	23%	34%	38%	50%
Construction	51%	60%	56%	47%	15%	23%	22%	27%
Type/keyboard	13%	15%	21%	34%	25%	39%	34%	37%
Computing	11%	18%	23%	41%	13%	24%	21%	31%
Providing care	21%	22%	17%	20%	64%	61%	54%	52%
Advice/Support	40%	44%	43%	57%	57%	59%	62%	58%
Teaching	23%	34%	33%	48%	46%	49%	52%	60%
Supervising others	37%	44%	49%	60%	36%	38%	42%	48%
Maths calculations	21%	34%	49%	68%	14%	36%	35%	51%
Selling products	21%	24%	26%	29%	23%	19%	20%	20%
Finance/accounting	17%	24%	29%	39%	12%	30%	33%	33%
Organisation	21%	32%	33%	39%	20%	20%	23%	26%
Comprehension	39%	54%	64%	78%	37%	65%	70%	77%
Decision Making	48%	58%	59%	68%	48%	54%	56%	51%
N =	(147)	(184)	(194)	272)	(239)	(249)	(223)	(189)

Promotion at Work

Getting training and acquiring skills are the necessary steps to the next stage of occupational achievement - promotion. Being promoted is a clear sign that your contribution at work is especially valued. Promotion is of course more common in some occupations than in others and will depend on a range of factors such as length of time in the job and in full-time employment generally, responsibilities exercised and so on (all of which men and women with poor skills fall short on). It was not surprising therefore to find that fewer men and women with poor skills had *ever* been promoted at work. Differences were, however, vast. As Figure 4.2 shows, between the ages 23 to 37, almost *two-thirds* of men and *three-quarters* of women with very low literacy skills had *never* been promoted. This compares with just under *one third* of men and just over *two fifths* of women with good literacy skills. With respect to numeracy ability among men this difference was reduced, but among women it was largely maintained: poor numeracy was just as much of a hindrance to women's promotion prospects as was poor literacy. The same differences occurred when the sample was restricted to people who had left full-time education at 16.

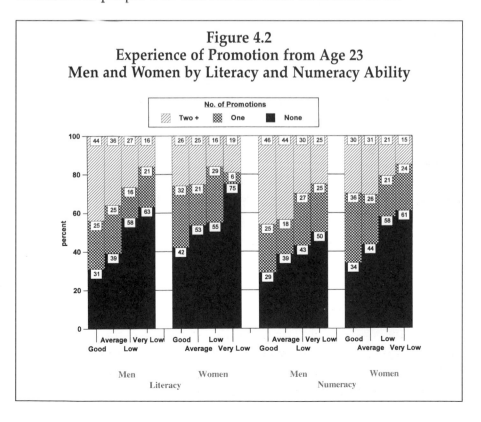

Figure 4.2
Experience of Promotion from Age 23
Men and Women by Literacy and Numeracy Ability

Earned Income

The final aspect of occupational achievement is the wages earned. As these are closely tied to type of occupation, we might expect occupation to account for a very large part of any variation in income between basic skills groups. Again to try to control at least some part of this effect we restrict analysis to those cohort members who left full-time education at 16. Figure 4.3 shows that far more men and women with poor skills than those with good skills had *low* incomes (under £200 for men, £150 for women). Although numbers were reduced in all groups, *twice* as many men in the very low numeracy groups earned a low income in comparison with men in the good numeracy group. The comparison for literacy showed 42% of those with very low and low literacy, earning low incomes, falling to 24% for those with good literacy. Among women, *over half* of those in the very low or low literacy and numeracy groups earned less than £150 per week, compared with 39% of women with good literacy skills and less than one-third of women in the good numeracy group.

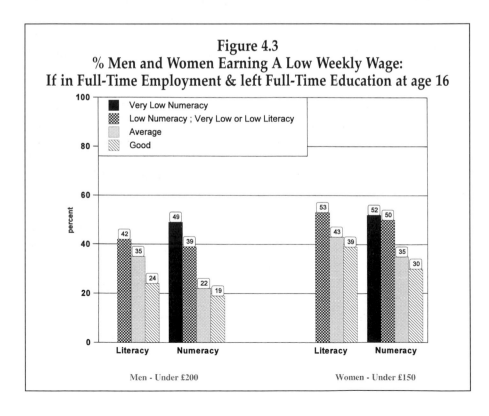

Figure 4.3
% Men and Women Earning A Low Weekly Wage:
If in Full-Time Employment & left Full-Time Education at age 16

Thus, even with groups equated for time of exposure to the labour market, basic skills difficulties appeared to impose an added disadvantage. The quality of family life is dependent to a certain extent on the level of household income, so we see indications now of the spread of disadvantage from the workplace to the home. We consider this feature of 37 year olds' basic skills difficulties in the next chapter.

Summary & Conclusions

People with poor basic skills generally had much more limited experience of work-based training, or courses leading to qualifications. They were more often in low paid, unskilled employment and had restricted opportunities for advancement. Often they were in jobs where opportunities for training were very limited. A further consequence was that far fewer in the poor basic skills groups reported possession of a wide range of work-related skills, some of which, such as computing and keyboard work, are central to modern employment prospects. The only skills in which those with poor literacy and poor numeracy estimated themselves as 'good' were 'ability to use tools' and 'construction' in the case of men, and 'providing care' in the case of women.

These last results are interesting as they point to the areas of the largely unregulated British labour market, where men without skills can still find work, ie. the building trades. Women with poor skills, on the other hand, have experience of caring skills from their more extensive experience of minding children or from work in jobs which involve caring.

Cohort members with poor basic skills were much less likely to have been promoted, and more likely to be in low income jobs. These differences held up even among samples of cohort members who had all left education at 16. So basic skills difficulties appear to lead to disadvantage in employment opportunities and prospects, over and above the effect of poor educational achievement.

CHAPTER 5

Family Life

Introduction

Although in the BCS70 survey some of the cohort members had married and started families, they were almost entirely early school leavers. More women had also taken this route than men. By 37 the majority of people that were likely to settle down with partners had done so. We can thus get a much better picture of the role of basic skills difficulties in family formation and breakdown from the older NCDS members.

Marriage and Cohabitation

The vast majority of men and women had married by age 37 or were cohabiting. Only 11% of men and 7% of women were single - either living alone or with other family members or friends. Those most likely to have *never* married or cohabited were men with poor skills: just under one fifth of those in the very low literacy or very low numeracy groups. Among the women, only those with very low literacy skills were more likely never to have married or to be cohabiting - 13% in comparison to 6-7% in the other basic skills groups.

Age of first marriage?

Men and women with poor skills had married at younger ages than the others. For example, the average age of first marriage for women in the very low literacy or very low numeracy groups was 23.5 years compared with 24.6 years and 24.9 years for women in the good literacy or good numeracy groups respectively. This earlier age of first marriage turned out to be related primarily to the earlier exit from education by the majority of men and women with poor skills - part of their generally accelerated transition to adulthood. When men and women who left full-time education at age 16 were compared, the differences between the basic skills groups disappeared.

Marital Breakdown ?

Does early entry into marriage and parenthood lead similarly to early marital breakdown? More women who had *ever been married* had experienced marital breakdown than men who had ever married (28% to 21% respectively). More of both sexes in the very low basic skills groups who had ever married had also experienced breakdown than those in the good skills groups. But again the earlier age at first marriage for women and the earlier exit from full-time education by men and women with poor skills accounted for most of these differences.

Of those who had left full-time education at 16, around one in three women had experienced a breakdown in their first marriage, regardless of literacy or numeracy ability. Similarly, less than one in four of ever married men in each numeracy group had experienced marital breakdown. For literacy, however, men with very low skills had a much higher experience of first marriage breakdown: 40% in comparison with just 16% of men with good literacy skills.

Children

Having children is typically contingent on marriage and cohabitation. Only 9% of men and 12% of women who were in their first marriage had not had any children by age 37. Inevitably, as *more* men with very low literacy or numeracy skills had not married and were not cohabiting at age 37, a slightly *higher* proportion of them were still childless by this age (ie. 30% with very low literacy skills compared with 24% with good literacy skills). For women, the opposite was found, just 10% with very low literacy had never had a child compared with 21% with good literacy. Much the same picture was evident for numeracy.

We now focus on men and women who had *any* children. In earlier work using BCS70 data at age 21, the majority of men and women had yet to become parents (93% men; 83% women). It was therefore only possible to establish differences in the *onset* of parenthood: women with poor skills were far more likely to have had a child by age 21 than their counterparts with good skills. Although some women continue to have children well into their forties, and some men much later than this, for the great majority child bearing will have been completed by age 37. It was therefore possible to see if men, and particularly women, with poor literacy or numeracy skills had different childbearing patterns, or a larger family size. We look first at *when* cohort members had their children, and then at the total *number* of children by age 37. Had earlier differences disappeared by this time?

Age at First Birth

The average age that women with very low literacy skills had their first child was 23.4 years - almost three years before the average age of 26.2 years for women with good literacy skills. Average age at first birth was actually highest at 27.2 years for women with good numeracy skills. Because of the relationship between age of leaving education and child bearing we restricted the analysis to those who left full-time education at 16. Figure 5.1 shows the average age at first birth for men and women in each of the literacy and numeracy groups. The average age of first birth was still two years younger for women within the very low literacy group in comparison with women in the good literacy group (22.2 years and 24.5 years respectively). A similar two year difference was also recorded for women who had left full-time education at 16 between the two extreme numeracy groups (23.4 years for women with very low skills, 25.3 years for women with good skills).

As for women, men's poor literacy was associated with early parenthood, but less strongly. The average age of first birth for men with very low or low literacy skills was 26 years in comparison with 28.2 years for men who had good literacy skills. Only a single year separated men by their numeracy ability. For men who left full-time education at age 16, the two years difference in age of first birth remained across the literacy groups. But for the numeracy groups there was no discernible difference.

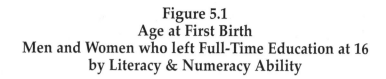

Figure 5.1
Age at First Birth
Men and Women who left Full-Time Education at 16
by Literacy & Numeracy Ability

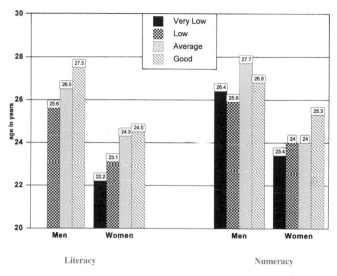

* small numbers dictated merging men with very low or low literacy skills.

Not only were poor literacy skills associated with early child bearing but also the number of children borne. For the majority who left full-time education at 16, poor literacy skills were again associated with increased childbearing. Figure 5.2 shows the percentages in each of the literacy groups who had one, two, three or four (plus) children by age 25.

Among women leaving school at 16, those with very low literacy skills were *three times* as likely to have had *3+ children* by age 25 in comparison with women with good literacy skills. (Notably, in the sample as a whole, women with very low literacy skills were *six times* as likely to have *3+ children* by the time they were 25). Men's tendency to father children later was reflected in much smaller numbers of children by age 25, and a much weaker relationship between basic skills proficiency and family size: 14% of men in the low literacy group had two children by the age of 25 compared with 8% of the good literacy group. The difference disappeared entirely for numeracy.

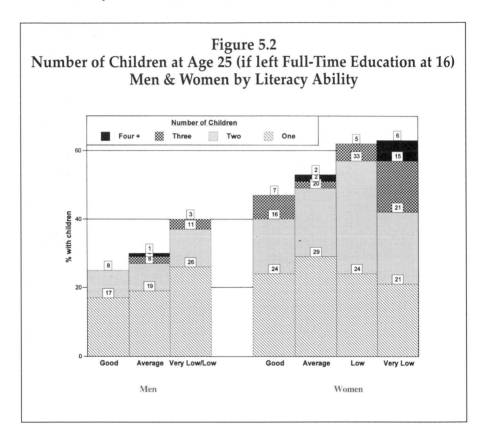

Figure 5.2
Number of Children at Age 25 (if left Full-Time Education at 16)
Men & Women by Literacy Ability

This pattern of child bearing across the basic skills groups continued to 37. Though for the men and women who had left school at 16, the proportions who had any children levelled off, the really large families of *4 plus* children were much more frequently to be found in the very low literacy skills group (12 % of men and 15% of women; 4% of men and 8% of women in the good literacy group). With respect to numeracy difficulties there were barely any differences in family sizes between groups.

Material Circumstances

Family income

In the previous chapter we noted the association between low wages and poor basic skills for people who were in full-time employment. But in many low income households either one or both partners is not active in the labour market, which reduces the overall family income even further. Restricting the analysis to men and women who were either married or cohabiting, was one or both partners in or out of paid employment?

Figure 5.3 shows the percentages of one non-earner, one part-time and two non-earner households in each of the four literacy and numeracy groups. It is clear that men and women with very low or low literacy and very low numeracy skills were *most* likely to be part of a non-earning household, and *least* likely to be working full-time

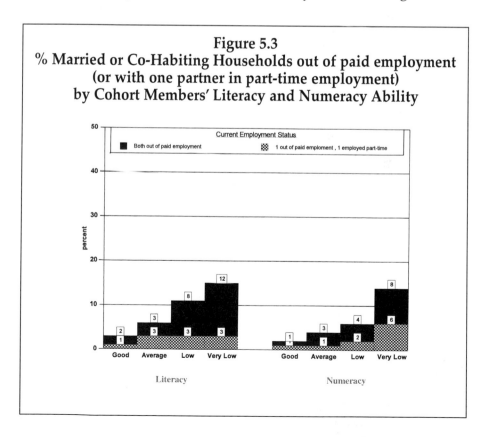

Figure 5.3
**% Married or Co-Habiting Households out of paid employment
(or with one partner in part-time employment)
by Cohort Members' Literacy and Numeracy Ability**

along with their partner. As many as 12% of married/cohabiting men and women with very low literacy skills and 8% of married/cohabiting men and women with low literacy or very low numeracy skills lived in a *non-earning* household. This compares with just 2% of men and women with good literacy skills and 1% of men and women assessed with good numeracy skills.

Housing

Earned income holds many implications for lifestyle and opportunity. A distinctive reflection of individual and family material prosperity is home ownership. We have established that far more men and women with below average literacy or numeracy skills earned a low income. They were also far more likely to live in *rented* council/housing association accommodation. Figure 5.4 shows the percentages living in different types of accommodation in each of the literacy and numeracy groups. Although two-thirds of men and women with very low literacy or very low numeracy skills owned

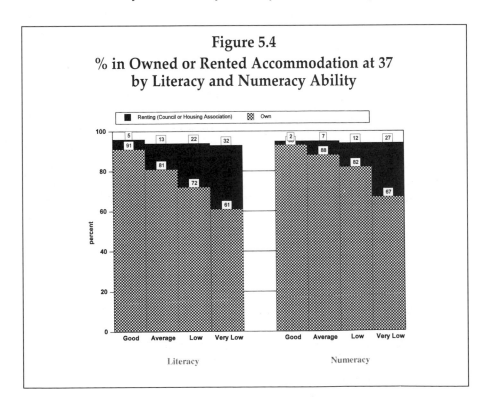

Figure 5.4

% in Owned or Rented Accommodation at 37 by Literacy and Numeracy Ability

their own home at age 37, this increased to over 90% for men and women with good skills. One third of men and women with very low literacy skills and 27% of those with very low numeracy skills were renting accommodation from their local council or housing association. 22% of women in the low literacy skills group also rented from their local council/housing association. Overall, gender differences were marginal.

Summary & Conclusions

In this chapter we have seen another side of the careers of people with poor basic skills. There were signs in the BCS70 survey of women with poor basic skills leaving the labour market early to have children. We now see other facets of the picture for an older sample in which most of those who are likely to have settled down and had children will have done so.

Men with poor basic skills were less likely to have married, but of the men and women in the poor basic skills groups, most of those who had married tended to have married much earlier than those without basic skills difficulties, and more had also experienced marital breakdown. But these outcomes appeared to be more associated with early school leaving than with any direct effect of basic skills problems. In other words the basic skills problem may have been implicated in poor educational attainments and early school leaving, but had no additional effect when people settled down with a partner. This was not the case for family size and age of having the first child. Even among cohort members who left school at 16, those with poor basic skills had far more children; three or more children were not uncommon. There are clear indications of the 'second career' taking over for these women (Hakim, 1996), ie. early exposure to the labour market and lack of satisfaction with the jobs found, leading to early exit from it and early childbearing.

The findings also reveal other indicators of stressful conditions surrounding family life. Thus despite the tendency towards large families, many of those families identified with poor basic skills had neither partner working. Low incomes and unemployment typically went with rented housing, usually from the Council. The picture overall was one of large families in poor material circumstances in which the basic skills problem was only one of a myriad of difficulties the family faced.

CHAPTER 6

Health and Participation in Public Life

Introduction

The previous chapter showed how basic skills difficulties tend to be associated with a relatively impoverished family life. In this final chapter we direct attention back to the individual in the two areas of health and public participation. Although social variations in health are well established, (eg. Fox and Goldblatt, 1990) and the poorly educated take less interest in public life than others, there is no one obvious reason why poor basic skills per se should show these connections. Only if the person's self esteem is affected by their awareness of basic skills problems, might we expect it to have an impact on their personal life and social participation.

Health and Well-Being

In fact, men and women with poor skills were far less likely to report *good* physical health over the past year. Differences were most apparent for men with respect to literacy ability. Over three quarters of men overall reported that they had been in good health over the previous year compared with half of those in the very low literacy group. Differences between groups were less pronounced for women: 72% of all women overall reported a good health status, compared with two thirds of women in the very low literacy and very low numeracy groups.

As noted in Chapter 1, cohort members also had their psychological well-being assessed by use of the Malaise Inventory (Rutter et al, 1970). Twenty-four *yes/no* questions elicited whether they were currently experiencing feelings of anxiety or depression. (The questions are shown in the Appendix). If 'yes' was answered to seven or more questions, a 'depressed' score was assigned. 7% of men and 11% of women were found to be 'depressed' overall.

Figure 6.1 shows striking differences between the basic skills groups in percentages registering as depressed, most notably for women. A massive 36% of women with very low literacy skills were designated by the test as depressed - *5 times* that of women with good literacy skills. For men the relationship was slightly weaker: three times as many men with very low literacy skills compared with men with good literacy skills scored 7 or more on the test. Differences were less pronounced for numeracy, but even so, women in the very low skills group were still *three times* as likely to be depressed, and men twice as likely, compared with those in the good numeracy skills group.

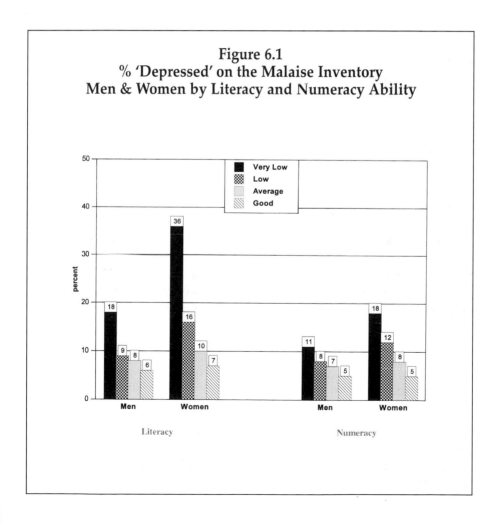

Figure 6.1
% 'Depressed' on the Malaise Inventory
Men & Women by Literacy and Numeracy Ability

Table 6.1a
Views and Outlook
Men and Women by Literacy Ability

	Men				**Women**			
	Very Low	Low	Average	Good	Very Low	Low	Average	Good
Satisfied with life so far	50%	76%	75%	78%	45%	65%	77%	76%
Never get what want from life	41%	24%	24%	18%	37%	26%	15%	14%
No control over events in life	23%	18%	11%	8%	10%	11%	8%	7%
Have to be careful who to trust	45%	38%	31%	23%	40%	20%	23%	22%
n=	(40)	(84)	(298)	(373)	(62)	(141)	(354)	(353)

Table 6.1b
Views and Outlook
Men and Women by Numeracy Ability

	Men				**Women**			
	Very Low	Low	Average	Good	Very Low	Low	Average	Good
Satisfied with life so far	64%	75%	73%	83%	61%	73%	79%	78%
Never get what want from life	35%	28%	21%	12%	29%	17%	12%	12%
No control over events in life	19%	13%	10%	6%	11%	8%	9%	6%
Have to be careful who to trust	40%	34%	28%	19%	27%	22%	24%	18%
n=	(147)	(184)	(194)	(271)	(240)	(248)	(224)	(189)

So, men and women with poor skills were more likely to report being in poor physical health, and far more were assessed to have symptoms of depression. Table 6.1a and Table 6.1b take this subjective assessment of well-being further. Far more men and women with very low or low literacy or numeracy skills were dissatisfied with their lives, and thought that life had not given them what they wanted. Satisfaction with life was reported least frequently by women with very low literacy skills (45%). More men with very low or low literacy or very low numeracy skills also reported that they felt *no control* over events in their life. Both men and women with poor skills were much less inclined to trust people: over 40% of men and women with very low literacy skills said they did not find it easy to trust people compared with 23% of the men and 22% of the women with good literacy skills.

Public Involvement

Information on public participation and organisation membership was collected in 1991, when cohort members were 33. The vast majority, 77% of men and 65% of women, had *never* been involved in *any* sort of organisation - whether it was political, a charity, residents' association, parent-teacher association, women's group, etc.

As Table 6.2a and Table 6.2b show, for literacy and numeracy ability respectively, women's increased involvement was largely accounted for by their greater involvement in parent-teacher association or charity work. The most involvement was recorded by men and women with good literacy or numeracy skills: one third of men and half of women had been a member of some public organisation at some time. Involvement was lowest for men and women with very low literacy skills: only 3% of men and 14% of women had *ever* been a member of a public organisation. This compared with 30% of men and 47% of women with good literacy skills.

On the political scene, just 6% of men and 4% of women had ever been a member of a political party: 3% of men and 2% of women were members in 1991. No women with very low or low literacy or very low numeracy skills had *ever* been a member of a political organisation. For men, only those with very low literacy skills had *never* been a member of a political organisation. (Although the percentage of men and women involved in any organisation was even lower when the sample was restricted to early school leavers, differences between groups were just as pronounced).

Table 6.2a
Organisation Involvement
Men and Women by Literacy Ability

	Men				**Women**			
	Very Low	Low	Average	Good	Very Low	Low	Average	Good
Any Organisation?	3%	11%	20%	30%	14%	21%	32%	47%
Political	0%	3%	6%	6%	0%	0%	4%	7%
Charity *(environment)*	3%	5%	6%	8%	4%	4%	6%	11%
Charity *(other)*	0%	7%	9%	9%	2%	7%	11%	22%
P.T.A.	0%	0%	4%	5%	6%	11%	16%	21%
n=	*(38)*	*(81)*	*(283)*	*(347)*	*(55)*	*(126)*	*(339)*	*(341)*

Table 6.2b
Organisation Involvement
Men and Women by Numeracy Ability

	Men				**Women**			
	Very Low	Low	Average	Good	Very Low	Low	Average	Good
Any Organisation?	11%	16%	25%	32%	22%	29%	43%	50%
Political	4%	6%	6%	6%	0%	3%	8%	6%
Charity *(environment)*	5%	2%	11%	8%	2%	6%	12%	10%
Charity *(other)*	5%	7%	10%	11%	6%	13%	19%	20%
P.T.A.	0%	3%	4%	6%	12%	15%	19%	22%
n=	*(138)*	*(175)*	*(179)*	*(258)*	*(216)*	*(237)*	*(216)*	*(183)*

Political Participation

Political interest?

Over 50% of men and one in three of women expressed an interest in politics overall. For those who left full-time education at 16, just 14% of men and 17% of women in the very low literacy group expressed an interest in politics compared with 53% of men and 33% of women with good literacy skills. Differences were as marked by numeracy ability for women, but political interest did not differ by numeracy ability for men.

Figure 6.2 shows that men and women with poor skills were also far more politically disillusioned. Around 1 in 4 women with very low skills agreed that "none of the political parties would do anything to benefit me" in comparison with 1 in 10 of women with good skills. For men, differences were even wider: 1 in 2 men with very low literacy skills and 1 in 3 men with very low numeracy skills held this view. This compared with approximately 1 in 10 men who had good literacy or good numeracy skills. (Differences did not diminish when the sample was restricted to early school leavers).

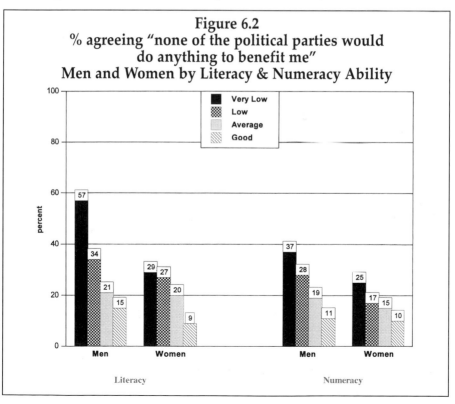

Figure 6.2
% agreeing "none of the political parties would do anything to benefit me"
Men and Women by Literacy & Numeracy Ability

More of those with poor skills also felt that they had no voice in the political decision-making process (in response to the question 'people like me have no say in what the government does'). Although 57% of all men and 47% of all women held this view, over 20% more of men and women with very low literacy or numeracy skills, and men with low literacy skills felt outside of the political arena in comparison with men and women who had good skills. Those most likely to feel a part of political decision-making were women with good numeracy skills (only 39% said they had no voice).

Voting

Although people may not take political interest and activity as far as joining a political party, most will vote in general elections (Heath and Topf, 1987). Cohort members were 18 in March 1976: three General Elections and numerous local elections had taken place between 1976 - 1991. Very few men and women (less than 10%) had

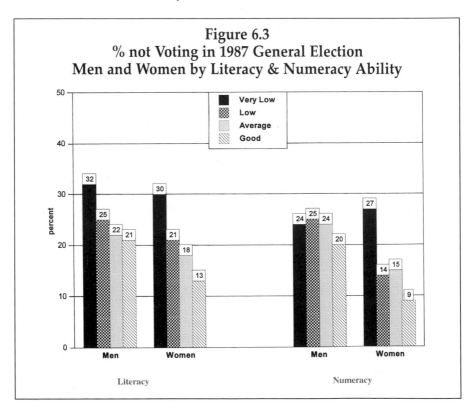

Figure 6.3
% not Voting in 1987 General Election
Men and Women by Literacy & Numeracy Ability

never voted in a national or local election. The proportion who had not voted increased in the very low skilled groups, being highest for women with very low literacy skills at 17%. At the General Election in 1987 a high *1 in 5* did not vote: 22% of men and 17% of women. As Figure 6.3 shows, those with very low literacy skills were least likely to have voted: 32% of men and 30% of women stayed away from the polling stations.

Differences between the basic skills groups in the proportions voting in 1987 were most pronounced for women. Women with very low literacy skills were more than *twice* as likely not to have voted compared with women who had good skills; women with very low numeracy skills were *three times* more likely not to have voted compared with women who had good numeracy skills. There were no discernible differences between the numeracy groups in the proportions of men voting. When the sample was restricted to early school leavers, virtually identical differences between groups were found, suggesting that the basic skills difficulties were exercising an independent effect on voting.

Summary & Conclusions

This final facet of basic skills difficulties brings us back to the individual: what effect were basic skills difficulties having on the cohort members' personal and public lives?

One striking finding was the much higher reporting among the very low literacy and numeracy groups of physical health problems. Substantially more of the cohort members with poor basic skills were also classified as depressed on the malaise scale - particularly women. The depressed state of people with very low literacy or very low numeracy was reflected further in expressions of dissatisfaction with life, poor self efficacy and lack of trust in people.

The overall picture was one of poor or reduced psychological state brought about by a tough, difficult, and in many respects a disappointing life. Though far more had clearly contributed to these cohort members' unhappiness than merely basic skills difficulties, there were strong signs of vicious circles of deprivation and disadvantage being set in motion, in which the basic skills problem had a major part.

The final expression of these difficulties was a lack of participation in politics and other areas of public life. Although such activity as membership of political parties was rare, the great majority of people voted in elections. However, among the very low basic skills groups, even this indicator of participation was missing for much larger numbers. Thus not only in the areas of working and domestic life were people with basic skills difficulties impoverished, but also in their role as citizens, through lack of participation in the political process.

CHAPTER 7

Basic Skills and Life Problems

The findings we have been examining in this report relate to 37 year olds at what might be called the prime of adult life. They point to an accumulating set of disadvantages for people with basic skills problems, the origins of which generally lie much earlier on in life. Emerging difficulties with basic skills at the beginning of primary school are followed by poor educational attainment at secondary school and leaving without qualifications (Bynner and Steedman, 1995). The transition from school to work presents another set of problems. Limited opportunities in the labour market force the early school leaver, first, typically, into a training scheme and then often into casual work interspersed with unemployment. In the case of young women early exit from the labour market, often to have children, is another common pattern. The question arises whether these life patterns are continuing or getting better or worse in succeeding generations. Are the new generations showing fewer signs of problems and adapting better to labour market conditions than their predecessors?

The Changing Context

To find out what is happening across the generations we can set our findings for the NCDS cohort against those for the BCS70 cohort, born 12 years later. The economic conditions were very different at the time the two sets of cohort members reached 16 and so their labour market experiences were likely to be different. For example, the BCS70 cohort were the first generation to face the almost complete collapse of the youth labour market in Britain (Banks et al,1992; Bynner, Wiggins and Parsons, 1996). More of the BCS70 cohort members stayed closer to education for longer. Compared with approaching two thirds of the NCDS cohort, who left school at 16, only half the BCS70 cohort similarly left education at the earliest possible age; (today it is about one third).

Although there are limitations in the comparisons one can make between the data - most obviously a different literacy and numeracy assessment was used in the two surveys - the questions asked about education, training, employment and family were the same or very similar, and up to the age of 23 covered the same period of life. Comparison between the two surveys can therefore give us some valuable insights into what was happening to young people especially in relation to the transition from school to work.

Skills problems

The distribution of literacy and numeracy scores was much the same in the two surveys. More people had problems with the harder tasks in literacy [excluding writing] whereas problems were more evenly spread in numeracy.

Although the tasks were different in the BCS70 and the NCDS literacy and numeracy assessment, the kinds of skills identified as difficult at each of the Wordpower and Numberpower levels were much the same. Extracting information from complex written text and graphical presentations were the most difficult literacy tasks for both men and women. With respect to numeracy, working out percentages, and using measurements in calculations, defeated large numbers, especially women.

There were some bigger differences between the two surveys in the reporting of specific problems. As we noted in Chapter 2, the BCS70 survey showed much the same levels of reported difficulty with one or more of the basics skills - if anything slightly more of the older (1958) cohort appear to have had problems - 13% (BCS70), 15% (NCDS). Of those in the NCDS survey who said they had difficulties, not being able to read a book to a child or to deal with formal paperwork were reported by up to 15%. Around twice this proportion said they could do the tasks, but only with difficulty. Corresponding percentages in the BCS70 survey for 'can't do' were all lower, never exceeding 10%. Fewer BCS70 cohort members also reported that they had problems recognising words (69% NCDS compared with 58% BCS70). On the other hand, probably reflecting their greater age and experience, fewer of the NCDS cohort members said they found difficulty in making sense of a piece of writing or concentrating on a piece of writing for long. Writing problems and spelling problems were also *less* frequently reported in the NCDS survey. Spelling, however, surfaced overwhelmingly, as the major problem in both surveys.

For numeracy much the same picture was apparent. The mathematical techniques presenting problems surfaced in identical order in the two surveys. The percentages reporting difficulty with dividing, subtracting, adding up and recognising numbers were 70%, 54%, 38%, 14% in BCS70 compared with 74%, 57%, 39% and 12% in the NCDS survey. It seems that the perception of numeracy problems persists at much the same level regardless of the respondent's age. With respect to every day use of numbers, again there was little difference. Only in relation to managing household accounts did *fewer* NCDS cohort members report a difficulty, presumably because they had more experience of this.

The results suggest that literacy and numeracy difficulties stabilise as people get older. The skills problems identified at age 21 remain as prevalent at age 37. There are few signs of either an improvement of these problems, as people get older, or further deterioration. Whatever has gone wrong in education that led to these difficulties in the first place, maintains its impact throughout adult life.

However, one notable difference between the two surveys was the cohort members' response to their own difficulties. As we noted in chapter 2 more of the NCDS cohort members who reported difficulties had attended a course to help them. As people get older, more take some remedial action for their basic skills problem. Having children may well be an important factor in this because of the added pressure it puts on the individual to help their child with school. This underlines the need to continue to target these older age groups for remedial basic skills teaching. The family literacy programme offers a particularly good opportunity to bring together parents' concerns about their own literacy needs with those of their children.

Education, employment and personal life

In chapter 3 we demonstrated how strongly poor basics skills are associated with low educational achievement. In the BCS70 survey this was similarly shown by the strong connection between competence in the basic skills and the school qualifications obtained - and following school those obtained from further education (Ekinsmyth and Bynner, 1994). However, the percentages gaining some kind of basic qualification were larger for the NCDS 37 year olds, suggesting that some had been able to get over the hurdle of poor basic skills to obtain qualifications - especially vocational qualifications. Thus by age 37, 31% of men and 27% of women in the very low literacy group had achieved a qualification up to the equivalent of 'O' Level', RSA Stage 2 or City and Guilds operative; 5% had reached the equivalent of 'A' Level or higher! In BCS70 none of the cohort members had reached this last level.

The poor educational attainment of people with basic skills problems carried over in both surveys into poor employment prospects. But there were signs that prospects were even worse in the BCS70 cohort. Thus in both surveys those with poor basic skills tended to leave school at the earliest age, and to have more difficulties than others in maintaining employment. However for the BCS70 cohort this was evident at the point of initial labour market entry. Most NCDS cohort members with poor basic skills gained some kind of job (though rarely apprenticeship) when leaving school. In consequence they had some employment experience behind them when the recession of the early 80s squeezed many of them out of their jobs. A much higher proportion of BCS70 cohort members failed to make the initial transition into a job, often finding themselves on dead-end training schemes or unemployed instead. Young men's subsequent careers were characterised by casual unskilled jobs or unemployment. Young women in this situation frequently left the labour market, often to have children. In BCS70, even at the relatively young age of 21, one third of females with poor literacy defined themselves as 'at home'. The same proportion of male respondents with poor literacy defined themselves as 'unemployed'.

Those who did find some kind of niche in the labour market shared with the NCDS cohort similar prospects. Their careers were marked by lack of work-based training opportunities, low income and poor promotion prospects. By age 37, most NCDS cohort members' careers had stabilised. Those with poor basic skills were mostly engaged in unskilled or partly skilled manual work , or were out of the labour market, unemployed or permanently 'sick'. The survey pointed to a compounding of labour market problems as they got older which shows how necessary remedial courses and training are to enable people in this situation to cross what often becomes a psychological, as well as a skills barrier, to getting a proper job.

In their personal lives the difficulties of adjustment to the demands of the labour market similarly appeared to be compounded with age. Thus the NCDS cohort members with poor basic skills showed relatively higher levels of depression than their counterparts in BCS70, especially among women, and showed many other features of low self esteem. Among men relatively high numbers were unmarried and without children. In contrast, women were more often characterised by early child bearing and early motherhood. One in five of the BCS70 women in the lowest literacy group had two or more children by the age of 20 , a figure which was replicated in the NCDS survey. In the NCDS survey by age 37 one in six of the very low literacy group had four or more children compared with one in twenty five men and one in twelve women in the good literacy group. Much of these differences can be accounted for by early school leaving which accelerates the transition into all areas of adult life. But lying at the core of this decision to leave education remains poor school achievement, often underpinned by a basic skills difficulty.

Basic Skills and Social Exclusion

As noted in the first chapter, an increasing concern in modern societies has been the marginalisation of certain sections of the population into low-grade and insecure work interspersed with periods of unemployment. Such employment experience is accompanied by sets of other disadvantages placing the individuals concerned increasingly on the periphery of the modern state. The term *social exclusion* is frequently used to describe the situation of what is a growing minority of people: a new underclass?

It becomes clear through this survey of 37 year olds that a necessary, if not altogether sufficient, condition to escape from the social exclusion trap is associated with basic skills. As the demand for extended education and training increases, so there is an added premium on the building blocks of educational achievement, and these are strongly connected with literacy and numeracy. The survey has shown that not only is educational achievement stunted through basic skills difficulties, but that access is very limited to the further education and training gained through employment that might rectify them. As they get older, people with basic skills difficulties have more and more difficulty in holding on to anything more than a marginal kind of job. Large proportions of women in this category give up the labour market altogether in favour of early childbearing and child-care. More men suffer broken marriages than their counterparts with good skills, and the marital lives of both men and women with skills difficulties are characterised by large families, and disadvantages in terms of low income and rented housing.

There are few personal pay-offs as compensation in this situation. The basic skills difficulty is accompanied by measurable levels of depression, and dissatisfaction with life generally, especially among women. Physical health is also reported as poor in comparison with people without basic skills difficulties. Finally, the role of *citizen* also appears to be damaged by a basic skills deficit in so far as citizenship can be measured by participation in public life and the likelihood of voting in an election. The degree of marginalisation experienced by people in these skills deficit groups is thus accentuated even further.

Numeracy problems appear to pose a particular difficulty for both sexes in relation to employment. Poor numeracy is associated with unemployment, lack of training and low income. On the other hand, in relation to promotion at work and the range of home and family attributes, health and forms of public participation associated with poor basic skills, with some exceptions, literacy appeared to be the more important factor. The significance of numeracy in modern employment has been highlighted in another report (Bynner and Parsons, 1997). The data presented here shows more facets of the disadvantages people with poor numeracy face. They also underline the continuing significance of literacy as an essential attribute in all areas of life.

The overriding conclusion to draw is that the situation revealed through these surveys poses huge problems not only for the individual concerned but for wider society. This is not to down play the adjustments many people are able to make to accommodate their basic skills difficulty. Many people are able to lead satisfying lives despite problems with literacy and numeracy. The statistical data generated by surveys do no more than reveal tendencies in a population. The striking feature of this survey is that the data points so consistently to an accumulation of disadvantage among people with poor basic skills.

The low levels of employment among men and women and the dependency on state benefits that this implies, is a burden on the modern state. It is not sensationalist to assume that the future will be even tougher for all concerned, but particularly for the men and women in succeeding generations who have not mastered the basic skills. From comparing the experiences of men and women with basic skills difficulties in NCDS and BCS70, we have to conclude that the difficulties associated with these problems have intensified over the years. Relatively speaking the entry of NCDS cohort members into the labour market was trouble free. By age 21 most were in some kind of employment. In contrast, substantial numbers in the BCS70 cohort who left education early had problems in establishing themselves in a job. Many spent a lot of their time on training schemes until unemployment finally took over. Thus although the men and women at age 37 in NCDS with basic skills difficulties compare *less* favourably in certain respects with their younger counterparts in BCS70, by the time the younger cohort reaches 37 we foresee problems on an even bigger scale for them. In a world where success in both the workplace and the home relies on an ever-increasing number of skills, we can only guess at how severe the exclusion of the younger cohort will be. Additionally, the children of the families in which these difficulties are occurring are themselves likely to start life with disadvantage and poor acquisition of basic skills at school. So the difficulties are repeated through the generations.

Although there are no cast iron predictions to be made about this, the dice is clearly loaded against these families and their children in so far as future opportunities are concerned. The case is clearly made for a continuing if not expanded effort to rectify at least one of the components of this disadvantage through the basic skills route. Remedial action to improve literacy and numeracy is not going to transform the lives of 37 year olds overnight, nor the lives of the cohorts that follow them, but it is going to give them at least one means by which they can seek the training and educational opportunities they have lacked in the past. It will also help them provide the educational environment at home, which is more conducive and supportive to their children's own educational achievement.

Finally we need to recognise that our identification of people with poor literacy and numeracy undoubtedly under estimates the size of the problem. This is because all longitudinal surveys suffer from attrition. People leave the survey as they get older. Disproportionately these tend to be located in the low achieving groups, including those with poor basic skills. This perhaps makes the case, as much as anything else we have said, for taking the basic skills issue seriously. A large, and perhaps growing, sub-class of people are getting increasingly out of step with the demands of the modern world. Only effective educational targeting offers the means of matching both their, and society's, needs.

References

ALBSU (Adult Literacy and Basic Skills Unit) (1987) *Literacy, Numeracy and Adults*. London: ALBSU

Ashton, D. and Maguire, M.(1986) *Young Adults in the Labour Market*. Department of Employment Research Paper, No 85, London: HMSO.

Beck, U. (1996) Risk Society. London: Sage.

Bynner, J. (in press) 'The transition from education to work: new routes to employment integration and exclusion' in Heinz, W. R. (ed.) *New passages from Education to Employment in Comparative Life Course Perspective*. Cambridge University Press.

Bynner, J. (1994) *'Skills and Occupations: Analysis of Cohort Members Self-reported skills in the Fifth sweep of the National Child Development Study.'* NCDS Working Paper, No 45, SSRU, City University.

Bynner, J. and Fogelman, K. (1993) Making the Grade: Education and Training, in Ferri, E. (ed.)Life at 33. London: National Children's Bureau.

Bynner, J. , Morphy, L., and Parsons, S.(1996) 'Women, Employment and Skills'. NCDS Users Support Group Working Paper No. 44, Social Statistics Research Unit, City University.

Bynner, J. and Parsons, S. (1997). *Does Numeracy Matter?* London: Basic Skills Agency

Bynner, J. and Steedman, J. (1995) *Difficulties with Basic Skills*. London: Basic Skills Agency.

ED (Employment Department) (1988) Employment for the 90s. Cm540, London: HMSO.

Ekinsmyth, C.; Bynner, J.; Montgomery, S. and Shepherd, P. (1992) *An Integrated Approach to the Design and Analysis of the 1970 British Cohort Study (BCS70) and the National Child Development Study (NCDS).* Inter-cohort Analysis Working Papers, No. 1 Social Statistics Research Unit City University.

Ekinsmyth, C. and Bynner, J. (1994)*The Basic Skills of Young Adults.* London: Basic Skills Agency.

Evans, K. and Heinz, W. (1994) *Becoming Adults in the 1990s.* London: Anglo German Foundation.

Goldblatt, P. and Fox, A.J. (1990) 'Mortality of Men by Occupation' in Goldblatt, P (Ed.) *Longitudinal Study: Mortality and Social Organisation,* Longitudinal Study Series no 6.110-129 London: HMSO.

Hakim, C. (1996) *Key Issues in Women's Work.* London: Athlone.

Heath, A. and Topf, R. (1987) 'Political Culture in British Social Attitudes', in Jowell, R., Witherspoon, S. and Brook, L. (eds.) *British Social Attitudes Survey,* the 1987 Report. Aldershot: Gower.

Jones, G. and Wallace, C. (1992) *Youth, Family and Citizenship.* Buckingham: Open University Press.

Joshi, H. and Hinde, P.R. (1993) 'Employment after Child Bearing in Post War Britain: Cohort study evidence on contrasts within and between generations'. *European Sociological Review,* 9, 203-227.

Rutter M., Tizzard, J. and Whitemore, K (1970) *Education, Health and Behaviour.* London: Longman.

Appendices

APPENDIX 1

Literacy 'Show Cards'

THE FIRM

Appearing at the

BIRMINGHAM NATIONAL
EXHIBITION CENTRE

On
19 November 1991
at
7.30pm

Tickets:
£8.50, £10.00, £15.00

Dear Pat,

As I am going to be late home from work today I would be very grateful if you could buy some items for me on your regular trip to the supermarket. I shall need:

> a large loaf of sliced brown bread
>
> a jar of marmalade
>
> a packet of cornflakes
>
> 1 pound of apples
>
> 1 packet (1 kg) of basmati rice
>
> 2 small plain yoghurts

I enclose £10.00 to cover the cost of these items.

I hope to see you at about 9 o'clock this evening.

Thank you very much for your kindness.

Jo

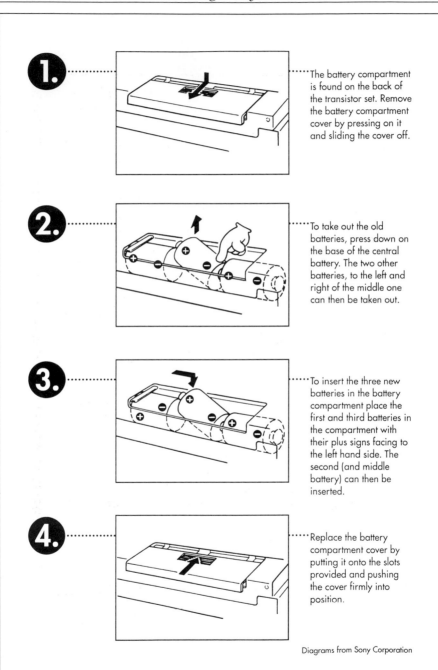

1. The battery compartment is found on the back of the transistor set. Remove the battery compartment cover by pressing on it and sliding the cover off.

2. To take out the old batteries, press down on the base of the central battery. The two other batteries, to the left and right of the middle one can then be taken out.

3. To insert the three new batteries in the battery compartment place the first and third batteries in the compartment with their plus signs facing to the left hand side. The second (and middle battery) can then be inserted.

4. Replace the battery compartment cover by putting it onto the slots provided and pushing the cover firmly into position.

Diagrams from Sony Corporation

The Stowaway Cat

Whisky the cat had only planned to curl up for a quick snooze after a night on the tiles in Louisville, Kentucky. She ended up nursing a bad hangover after spending thirty days in a used whisky barrel while crossing the Atlantic Ocean by ship.

The young black and white cat survived without food by licking the dregs from the wooden barrel. When she walked unsteadily into the whisky distillery in Keith, Scotland, she was very much the worse for wear.

"She was struggling to get to her feet, not just through lack of food, but because she would also have been somewhat affected by the whisky", said company boss John Watson.

The police, who were called to look into this unlawful entry, said cat stowaways are usually destroyed. But the company decided to spare what was left of Whisky the cat's nine lives.

"It seemed the only decent thing to do after all she has been through. It's amazing that she's still alive."

Whisky is now serving out her time in a cattery. She had lost weight during the journey by ship but was able to get vital nourishment from the whisky dregs.

Adapted from report by Angelia Johnson
The Guardian, 17.6.93

1003

Classification index   P

1008

Classification index V/W

PLUMBERS   817

PLUMBING PROBLEMS?
- BURST PIPES TANKS • CENTRAL HEATING
- BOILER DIAGNOSIS • DRAINS

ONE HOUR EMERGENCY SERVICE

24 HOUR A DAY, 7 DAYS A WEEK
RING ANYTIME

**ALL WORK GUARANTEED
FOR ONE YEAR MINIMUM**

ALL PRICES AGREED IN ADVANCE

081-998 3540/081-998 6372

001 AALECTRON PLUMBING
CORGI REGISTERED MEMBER NO 17802
SUPERTRON LTD, MEM FEDERATION
OF MASTER BUILDERS
19/21 FOSSE WAY, EALING W13 0BZ
(Approved Dealer – Access/Visa/Amex)

101 A. Albert Plumbing & Heating,
291 Alexandra Avenue, Harrow HA2 ....081-423 7452
081-840 3221
071-431 8558
24 Hour Plumbing & Heating Co.
Bystan House, 1a Elystan Place, SW3 ....071-731 7597
071 Plumbing, 15 Nevern Rd, SW5 ....071-373 7052
A1 Fast Plumbing & Heating Service,
100 Fortune Green Rd, NW6 ....071-794 0363

A.C. CHAULK
General Plumbing Heating & Bathrooms
44 Byron Rd,
Wembley, HA0 3PD 081-904 5413

AC Contractors,
11 Stapenhill Rd, Wembley, HA0 ....081-904 3502

A.J.C.
All Types-Plumbing & Central Heating
25 Hartswood Road
London W12 ....081-740 5171

---

001 A. ANDREWS
EST 1977
**EMERGENCY PLUMBING
BOILER SPECIALISTS**
BURST PIPES + BOILERS REPAIRED
DRAIN CLEANING
LOWEST HOURLY RATES
WE NEVER CLOSE

081-575 2491

11 ST. PETERS ROAD, SOUTHALL

1A AEC PLUMBERS
**EALING, ACTON
& CHISWICK**
1 HOUR INSTANT SERVICE

- BURST PIPES
- BLOCKED DRAINS
- CENTRAL HEATING ETC

**081-998 8412
081-998 5600**

74 MADELEY ROAD, EALING W5

1st CALL
IMMEDIATE BUILDING REPAIRS

(0895) 624200

24 HOUR IMMEDIATE RESPONSE
All Small Electrical Repairs
Commercial and Domestic
General Electrical Work, Alarm Systems

Head Office: 348 Chaddow Rd, Bristol BS1 6PT

DIAL A DRAIN

NO CALL OUT CHARGE

- FIXED PRICE
- WRITTEN GUARANTEE

SINKS, TOILETS, DRAINS UNBLOCKED

FOR FAST LOCAL SERVICE CALL	
STANMORE	081-845 8106
RICKMANSWORTH	0923 211525
RUISLIP	0895 623466
HARROW	081-845 8106
HAMMERSMITH	081-741 7760
HAMPSTEAD	071-431 4431
FULHAM	071-351 2346
CHISWICK	081-943 4525

OR DIAL FREE 0800 501201

A.A.A. ABBOTT LTD, 2 Manor Rd, Middx HA4 7LA

---

24 HOUR PLUMBING SERVICE

**TOILETS • TANKS • TAPS • LEAKS • BURSTS
BOILERS • RADIATORS • PUMPS • BLOCKED DRAINS
WASTE DISPOSAL UNITS • IMMERSION HEATERS • BALL VALVES**

**NO CALL OUT
CHARGE**
•
**ALL WORK
GUARANTEED**
•
**£2 MILLION
PUBLIC
LIABILITY**

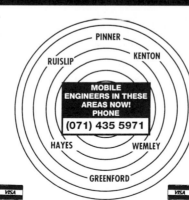

PINNER
RUISLIP
KENTON

**MOBILE
ENGINEERS IN THESE
AREAS NOW!
PHONE
(071) 435 5971**

HAYES
WEMLEY
GREENFORD

**A PLUMBER WITHIN
THE HOUR**

0 0 0 0 AA ABBOTT SERVICES
Unit 2, 336 Battersea Park Road
Battersea, London SW11 5AP

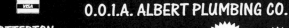

LOOK FOR THESE SIGNS OF COMPETENCE AND RESPONSIBILITY

Those listed below are a selection of IOP Registered Plumbers and Companies who undertake to carry out work to high standards

The Institute of Plumbing, 64 Station Lane, Hornchurch, Essex RM12 6NB

CHISWICK
*J. Skinner, RP
  J. Skinner Plumbing & Heating
  2 Winston Walk
  Acton Green
  W4 5SN   081-995 4135
           Cellnet (0860) 822285

EDGWARE
L.R. Gold, Eng Tech MIP RP
  L.R. Gold (Plumbing & Heating)
  54 Farm Road HA8 9LT   081-958 9300

*M.H. Luke, RP
  All-Ways (Emergency)
  111 Beverley Drive   081-952 5200
  HA8 5NI I   Cellnet (0860) 462008
  Plumbing, Heating & Cleaning Services incl Boiler &
  Saniflo Maintenance. CORGI Registered

D.W. Smith, RP
  186 Broadfields Avenue
  HA8 8TF   081-958 3868

FULHAM
R.W. Barron, Eng Tech MIP RP
  Barron Building Services
  92 Stephendale Road
  SW6 2PQ   071-731 2561

A.D. Williams, RP
  A.D. Williams Plumbing & Heating
  57 Cuckoo Avenue
  W7 1BW   081-578 5237

HARROW
P.L. Brown, Eng Tech MIP RP
  Peter Brown Plumbing & Heating Contractors
  Unit 3
  29/31 Frognal Avenue
  HA1 2SG   081-863 1155
  Industrial Domestic And Contract Work

*M.J. Greenyer, AIP RP
  M. & M. Plumbing & Heating
  115 Leamington Crescent 081-864 6827
  HA2 9HJ   Vodafone (0831) 320248

*A.A. Marshall, RP
  A.A. Marshall (Plumbing & Heating)
  17 Twyford Road   081-422 0979
  HA2 0SH   081-205 6283

*W.P. Murray, RP
  W. Murray & Associates
  54 Headstone Road   081-863 3824
  HA1 1PE   Vodafone (0836) 549962
  Specialists in Domestic Plumbing and Heating Gas
  Installations

*A.S. Patel, RP
  A.P. Plumbing
  11 Carlyon Avenue
  HA2 8SN   081-422 2145

*J.A. Sumner, RP
  L.H. Plumbing & Heating Services Ltd
  132-134 Vaughan Road
  HA1 4ED   081-864 2311

HAYES
J.F. Heppelthwaite, MIP RP
  J.F. Heppelthwaite Ltd
  Caxton House
  Printing House Lane   081-756 1608
  UB3 1AP   081-573 9410
  Heating Installation, Servicing & Repairs,
  Domestic & Commercial Housing Assoc. Schools

*M.J. Williams, RP
  M.J. Williams & Son
  25 Glamas Crescent   081-561 6509
  UB3 1QA   Vodafone (0836) 552904

ISLEWORTH
*J.G. Fielder, RP
  53 Talbot Road   081-892 3088
  TW7 7HG   Vodafone (0831) 336883

KINGSBURY
G.F. Mcmullan, RP
  G.M. Plumbing & Heating Co
  32a Leith Close
  Kingsbury   081-205 5280
  NW9 8DE   Cellnet (0860) 519741

NW2
D. Cheese, RP
  David Cheese Plumbing & Heating
  71 Prayle Grove
  Cricklewood NW2 I BB 081-450 9290

NW6
*D. Sanford, MIP RP
  Sanden Plumbing Co Ltd
  202 West End Lane
  Hampstead NW6 1SG   071-794 0064

NW7
M.P. Rudd, RP
  Rudd Engineering Ltd
  12 Fernside Avenue
  NW7 3BD   081-959 8181

NW9
*J.F. Green, MIP RP
  J.F. Green Plumbing & Heating Engineer
  42 Mallard Way   081-205 0486
  Kingsbury NW9 8JH Vodafone (0831) 832770
  Any Make – Gas Boiler Serviced/Repaired/Replaced

NW10
G.R. Beirens, RP
  Walkerfern
  97 Leigh Gardens
  NW10 5HN   081-960 6787

SW6
*T.C. Anderson, AIP, RP
  Anderson & Sons
  25 Filmer Road
  Fulham SW6 7BP   071-381 3784
  Showers, Pumps, Wash Machines, Combination Boilers
  Installed, Burst Pipes, Block Drains, 24 Hr Emerg.

W5
P.D. Corsini, RP
  Berkley Plumbing & Heating
  20 Freeland Road   081-992 2908
  W5 3HR   Vodafone (0836) 634043
  Plumbing, Heating, Drainage & Leadwork

*Anthony Halvey, RP
  Ash Services
  37 Cumberland Road
  W7 2ED   081-566 2967
  Bathroom Design & Installation

W12
*D.A. Coughlan, RP
  Anthonies Plumbing & Heating Contractor
  20 Foxglove Street
  Shepherds Bush, W12 8OD 081-749 6695

NEASDON
*S.M. Gorsia, RP
  Plumbing & Heating
  60 Ballogie   081-452 7417
  NW10 1SY   Mobile (0374) 132652

NORTHOLT
*B.A. Bennett, RP
  Harrow Plumbing
  28 Millway Gardens UB5 5DX 081-841 7248
  Any Emergency – Phone Cellnet (0860) 588099

*J.H. Davies, AIP RP
  Express Plumbing & Drainage
  64 Aspen Lane   081-841 5094
  UB5 6XH   081-579 5765

NORTHWOOD
*S.R. Curtis, AIP RP
  London & Home Counties Ltd
  72 High Street
  HA6 1BL   (0923) 821262

*I.F. Keene, AIP RP
  Plumbing & Central Heating Services
  67 Stanley Road
  HA6 I RJ   (0023) 826076
  CORGI Registered

RICKMANSWORTH
*G. Maddison, AIP RP
  51 Frankland Road
  Croxley Green WD3 3AS (0923) 770167

D.A.W. Stratford, RP
  213 Baldwins Lane
  WD3 3LH   (0923) 775600

*E.A. Tack, RP
  E.A. Tack, Plumbing & Heating
  13 The Greenway
  WD3 2HX   (0923) 778144

RUISLIP
J.F. Flynn, RP
  J.F. Flynn & Son Plumbing Contractors
  16 Evelyn Avenue   (0895) 631238
  HA4 8AS   081-569 1670

SOUTH HARROW
S.R. Newton, RP
  162 Roxeth Green Avenue
  HA2 0QW   081-423 3090

SOUTHALL
*K.K. Madar, RP
  K.M. Plumbing
  75 Ranelagh Road   081-843 9365
  UB1 1DJ   Cellnet (0860) 887175

UXBRIDGE
*A. Callaby, AIP RP
  A.C. Home Services
  41 Church Road UB8 3NO (0895) 259178
  Domestic Commercial Industrial Plumbing/Heating

M.J. Fryer, RP
  Fryer Plumbing Services
  142 Windsor Avenue
  Hillingdon UB10 9BO   (0895) 255435

G.S. Weekes, RP
  F & G Weekes
  180 Grosvenor Crescent
  Hillingdon UB10 9EZ   (0895) 259326

WEST DRAYTON
*M.E. Connolly, RP
  Connolly Plumbing Services
  17 Philpot's Close   (0895) 449452
  UB7 7RY   Mobile (0831) 690564

*Emergency Service

The following article recently appeared in a conservation magazine.

The Importance of Cereal Grasses in Providing Essential Food

THE grass family is one of the most important plant groups in the world. It is a major source of food for humans and animals, and grows with the least encouragement. It helps to prevent topsoil being worn away by the rain and wind. Many people do not realise that there are about 10,000 different species of grass in the world. They can be divided into six main groups: cereals, grazing grasses, sugar cane, turf, ornamental, and woody grasses.

Our need for cereal grasses is very large. Cereal grasses cover over half of the land used to grow food in the world. Cereals include things such as wheat, rice, maize, barley oats and rye. The seeds of wheat make grain which is ground into flour for making bread, noodles, pasta and breakfast cereals. Rice is the staple food for over a third of the world's population. Oats and maize are used to feed animals as well as humans. Oats are used to make things such as porridge, and maize is

Wheat

Wheat plants have upright ears which grow close together to make a compact head. Grain is removed from the ears of wheat and ground into flour for bread and pasta.

Barley

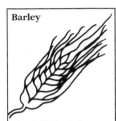

A head of barley is shorter than a head of rye and has loose ears and long "beards". When the ear is ripe it will hang down. When barley is sprouted and then dried, it becomes malt.

Rye

This looks similar to wheat except that the ears are extended by long "beards". Rye grows well on poor, sandy soil.

Maize or corn

Maize is grown in long rows. It has broad green leaves and can grow to over a metre in height. It is grown mostly for animal feed.

eaten in the forms of flour, sweetcorn, popcorn, and oil.

Large areas of grassland cover every continent. Almost half of the British landscape consists of grassland. About half of that is taken up with growing cereals. Some grasses simply help prepare land for cereal crops because they help to improve the structure of the soil.

WASHINGTON NEW TOWN

WASHINGTON, County Durham, was planned as a new town in 1964. At that time local unemployment was considered high at 4.5% as a result of a decline in coal mining, shipbuilding and heavy industries.

However, in the period 1965-1982 the population nearly trebled as new employers sought workers. One of the biggest employers, Nissan the motor manufacturers, built their new factory just outside the new town boundary. Firms that supplied parts to Nissan set up in Washington itself.

Of those in employment 44% worked in the new town, while the remainder had jobs outside. More than a third of the workers, who lived in the town, walked to work – a tribute to the new town planners who had provided pedestrian walkways.

Where people work in Washington, and what kinds of job

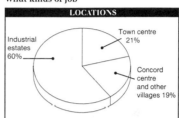

LOCATIONS

Industrial estates 60%

Town centre 21%

Concord centre and other villages 19%

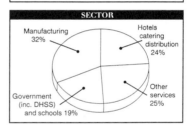

SECTOR

Manufacturing 32%

Hotels catering distribution 24%

Other services 25%

Government (inc. DHSS) and schools 19%

Washington new town statistics

Year	Population	New Dwellings	New factory space (m2)
1965	20,000	59	–
1966	20,298	142	–
1967	20,483	88	–
1968	21,182	333	19,942
1969	22,856	797	42,013
1970	23,623	365	63,822
1971	25,200	1061	12,701
1972	28,566	1603	59,624
1973	30,609	973	13,730
1974	33,120	1023	28,265
1975	37,900	1238	38,960
1976	41,500	1668	55,051
1977	46,565	1047	17,750
1978	47,733	685	4,598
1979	49,620	595	11,291
1980	50,100	908	57,833
1981	51,960	952	25,030
1982	52,570	937	24,060

Households & Families

Marriage and divorce

In recent decades most European countries have experienced considerable social change. These changes have been reflected in various demographic indicators, such as marriage, divorce and cohabitation. Generally speaking, in most European countries the prevalence of divorce and cohabitation has risen, whilst marriage rates have declined. Chart 1, which looks at marriage and divorce rates in Great Britain over the past two decades, shows that marriages have fallen by almost 16 per cent, whilst divorces have more than doubled over the same period.

In 1991, the number of divorces was over 171 thousand – the highest on record. For every two marriages in Great Britain in 1991 there was one divorce.

Households

Since 1945, there has been a large increase in the number of people living alone. Whilst the number of one person households has been growing, the number of 'traditional' households has been falling.

The most common household type in Great Britain is a married couple without children. One family households with between one or two children, or no children at all, comprise almost half the households in each country.

Families

Whereas a household is defined as a person living alone or a group of people living together, a family is a married, or cohabiting, couple with or without children, or a lone parent with children. People living alone are not considered a family. Between 1961 and 1992 there was a threefold increase in the proportion of people living alone and a fourfold increase in the proportion of the population living in lone parent families (compare Chart 2).

There were about 1.3 million one-parent families in Great Britain in 1991, containing approximately 2.2 million dependent children. In the four years up to 1991 the number of single parents grew, increasing by 24 per cent, while the number of dependent children in one-parent families increased by half a million, from 1.7 million in 1987. In 1991 just over 17 per cent of families with dependent children were headed by a lone mother compared with just over 1 per cent headed by a lone father (Chart 3). The figures reflect the rise in both divorce and births outside marriage.

1. Marriages and divorces

Great Britain
Thousands

Marriages

Divorces[1]

1. Including annulments

1971   1976   1981   1986   1991

Source: Office of Population Censuses and Surveys; General Register Office (Scotland)

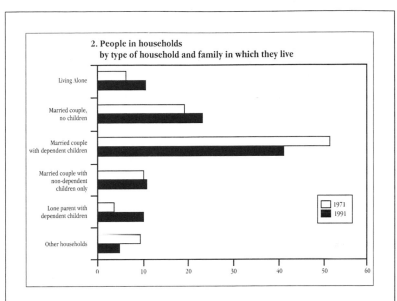

2. People in households
by type of household and family in which they live

- Living Alone
- Married couple, no children
- Married couple with dependent children
- Married couple with non-dependent children only
- Lone parent with dependent children
- Other households

☐ 1971
■ 1991

0   10   20   30   40   50   60

3. Families headed by lone mothers and lone fathers as a percentage[1] of all families with dependent children.

Great Britain

Percentages

All lone parents

Lone fathers

Lone mothers

1976   1981   1986   1991

1. Three-year moving average used (apart from 1991)
Source: Office of Population Censuses and Surveys

The number of births outside wedlock has increased dramatically since 1960. Even over the last decade, the proportion of live births outside marriage more than doubled to almost one in every three births in 1992 (Chart 4).

4. Live births outside marriage as a percentage of all births.

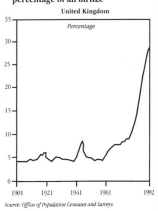

United Kingdom

Percentage

35
30
25
20
15
10
5
0

1901   1921   1941   1961   1992

Source: Office of Population Censuses and Surveys

Numeracy 'Show Cards'

SHOPPING FOR A NEIGHBOUR

a loaf of bread

68p each

two tins of soup

45p each

PLANNING A ROUTE FOR A JOB INTERVIEW

Hazledene & Co.

The Dene, Almsford, Hampshire.

Interview Details:

Interview time: 11.30

Please arrive by: 11.15

Hazledene & Co are a 10 minute walk from Almsford Railway Station.

British Rail ⇌   Timetable

Morton to Turnerstone   **Mon-Fri**

Morton	10.17	10.37	10.57	11.17
Graves End	10.21	10.41	11.01	11.21
Newgate	10.32	10.52	11.12	11.32
Appleby	10.40	11.00	11.20	11.40
Meadstone	10.49	11.09	11.29	11.49
Almsford	10.55	11.15	11.35	11.55
Turnerstone	11.01	11.21	11.41	12.01

Turnerstone to Morton   **Mon-Fri**

Turnerstone	12.24	12.59	13.34	13.59
Almsford	12.30	13.05	13.40	14.05
Meadstone	12.36	13.11	13.46	14.11
Appleby	12.45	13.20	13.55	14.20
Newgate	12.53	13.28	14.03	14.28
Graves End	13.04	13.39	14.14	14.39
Morton	13.08	13.43	14.18	14.43

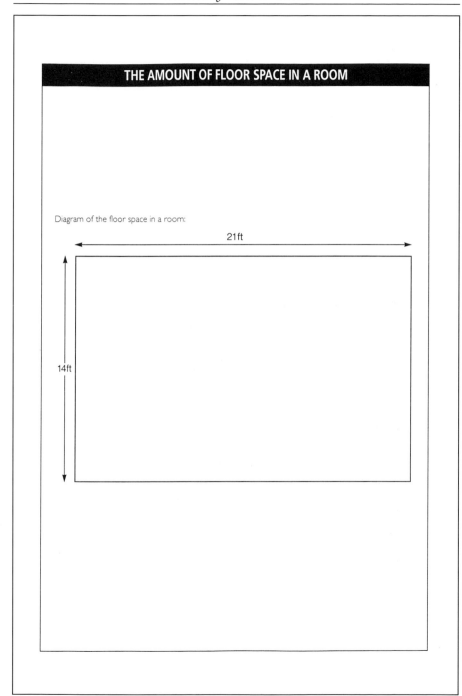

THE AMOUNT OF FLOOR SPACE IN A ROOM

Diagram of the floor space in a room:

21ft

14ft

WORKING OUT THE AMOUNT OF POND LINER REQUIRED

1. Measure the greatest length and
   the greatest width.

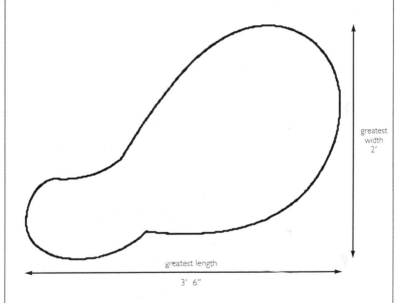

greatest
width
2'

greatest length

3' 6"

2. (a) To the greatest width add 2ft plus the depth of the
   pond.

   (b) To the greatest length add 2ft plus the depth of the
   pond.

3. Use (a) and (b) to calculate the area of the liner
   required.

CITY COUNCIL SPENDING 1993 AND 1994 (£ MILLION)

DEPARTMENT	1993 (£m)	1994 (£m)
EDUCATION	23.73	24.28
HOUSING	6.24	5.96
CLEANSING	2.16	2.87
FIRE	1.99	2.31
POLICE	8.80	10.34
AMBULANCE	2.85	3.02
OTHER	6.50	10.25
TOTAL	52.27	58.85

ORDER

Service chart at 12½%

Family 1 orders:

2 x Steak & Chips   £4.95 each

2 x Fish & Chips   £3.95 each

1 Bottle of White Wine   £4.90 each

3 x Ice Cream   £0.95 each

1 x Chocolate Pudding   £1.60 each

Family 2 orders:

1 x Steak & Chips   £4.95 each

2 x Fish & Chips   £3.95 each

1 Bottle of Red Wine   £4.99 each

3 x Ice Cream   £0.95 each

Bank Loan Rate Table

LOAN	60 month term		48 month term		36 month term		24 month term		12 month term	
	Monthly Repayment	Total Payable	Monthly Repayment	Total Payable	Monthly Repayment	Total Payable	Monthly Repayment	Total Payable	Monthly Repayment	Total Payable
1000	26.01	1560.60	29.97	1438.56	36.72	1321.92	50.47	1211.28	92.22	1106.64
1500	39.02	2341.20	44.95	2157.60	55.08	1982.88	75.71	1817.04	138.33	1659.96
2000	52.02	3121.20	59.94	2877.12	73.44	2643.84	100.94	2422.56	184.44	2213.28
2500	62.72	3763.20	72.70	3489.60	89.68	3228.48	124.13	2979.12	228.53	2742.36
3000	75.26	4515.60	87.24	4187.52	107.61	3873.96	148.96	3575.04	274.24	3290.88
4000	100.35	6021.00	116.33	5583.84	143.48	5165.28	198.61	4766.64	365.65	4387.80
5000	125.44	7526.40	145.41	6979.68	179.35	6456.60	248.26	5958.24	457.06	5484.72

Hire Purchase Loan Rate Table

	LOAN	£500	£2,000	£2,500	£5,000	£10,000
12 MONTHS	Total to repay £	555.96	2223.60	2755.08	5436.12	10872.12
	Monthly repayment £	46.32	185.30	229.59	453.01	906.01
24 MONTHS	Total to repay £	611.04	2443.68	3005.04	5859.84	11719.68
	Monthly repayment £	25.46	101.82	125.21	244.16	488.32
36 MONTHS	Total to repay £	669.24	2676.96	3268.44	6303.96	12607.92
	Monthly repayment £	18.59	74.36	90.79	175.11	350.22
48 MONTHS	Total to repay £	730.56	2923.20	3545.76	6768.00	13536.00
	Monthly repayment £	15.22	60.90	73.87	141.00	282.00
60 MONTHS	Total to repay £	795.60	3181.80	3835.80	7251.60	14503.20
	Monthly repayment £	13.26	53.03	63.93	120.86	241.72

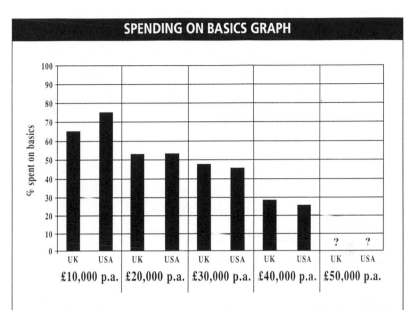

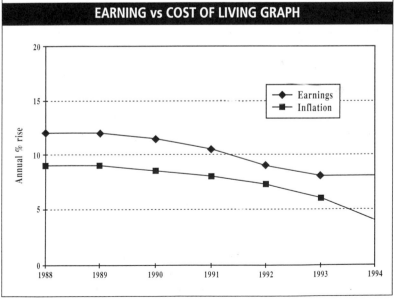

Table A1:   % Men and Women who answered
             Literacy Questions incorrectly by
             Literacy Ability

Table A2:   % Men and Women who answered
             Numeracy Questions incorrectly by
             Numeracy Ability

Table A3:   The Malaise Inventory, (Rutter et al, 1970)

Table A1
% Men and Women who answered Literacy Questions incorrectly by Literacy Ability

QUESTIONS	Men			Women		
	Very Low	Low	Average/ Good	Very Low	Low	Average/ Good
FOUNDATION LEVEL	%	%	%	%	%	%
1. A newspaper advert for a Concert...						
a. *Where was the concert being held ?*	33	13	3	29	11	3
b. *Who will be playing the concert ?*	3	1	0	10	0	<1
2. A letter was given to read...						
a. *What does Jo want Pat to do for her ?*	15	12	2%	11	6	2
b. *Why does she ask Pat to do shopping ?*	25	9	2%	15	7	1
c. *What time does Jo expect to return ?*	8	5	1%	8	1	1
3. Instructions for replacing a battery...						
a. *Where is the battery compartment found ?*	5	6	<1	16	4	<1
b. *Which of the old batteries should be removed first ?*	8	14	2	39	23	9
c. *Which of the three batteries should be inserted first ?*	18	15	4	45	33	6
LEVEL 1						
1. Reading a newspaper extract about a cat (Whisky)...						
a. *What was Whisky's condition ?*	70	58	28	69	47	23
b. *How did she survive without food ?*	28	19	4	45	9	5
c. *Where is Whisky now ?*	30	13	3	21	6	2
2. Consulting Yellow Pages...						
a. *From the index pages, which page are details of plumbers on ?*	68	48	15	68	49	15
b. *What is the telephone number of a Plumber in Chiswick ?*	38	11	2	39	14	1
LEVEL 2						
1. Reading a Conservation Article						
a. *How many types of grass are there in the world ?*	28	7	4	36	18	6
b. *Names of 3 types of cereal ?*	33	18	5	45	13	2
c. *Which cereal grows well in poor, sandy soil ?*	78	33	9	82	39	9
d. *How is flour made from wheat ?*	65	42	10	61	27	7
2. Reading Information about a Town...						
a. *In which year during 1965-1982, was the most new factory space available ?*	80	48	10	89	48	14
b. *What % of people work in the Town Centre ?*	75	37	11	84	58	11
c. *How do we know that the pedestrian walkways are successful ?*	75	35	7	77	36	6
LEVEL 3						
1. 'True' or 'False' to an article on Households and Families						
a. *Between 1971 - 1991, the number of divorces more than trebled.*	83	53	13	92	74	22
b. *Since 1971 there was a decrease in people who live alone.*	83	44	10	81	47	11
c. *In 1991, over 17% of families with children were headed by a lone mother.*	70	33	7	55	18	8

Table A2
% Men and Women who answered Numeracy Tasks incorrectly by Numeracy Ability

QUESTIONS	Men			Women		
	Very Low	Low	Average/ Good	Very Low	Low	Average/ Good
FOUNDATION LEVEL	%	%	%	%	%	%
1.Doing Shopping for a neighbour...						
a. How much change should you give after shopping ?	55	33	13	55	29	11
2. Planning a route for a job interview...						
a..Which train should you catch to arrive at the company in time ?	57	31	7	46	25	3
b. What time will you arrive at the company ?	77	47	14	76	39	8
3. Amount of Floor Space in a room...						
a. Calculate the area of a room in square feet.	73	29	9	84	57	17
LEVEL 1						
1. Ordering a Pizza with friends...						
a. What is the total cost ?	29	13	2	35	9	2
b. How much does each person have to pay ?	48	19	4	52	10	5
2. Digging a garden pond...						
a. What is the area of pond liner required ?	99	77	34	99	89	48
3. Information on Council Spending from a Chart...						
a. What was the 1993 Education spending to the nearest £1 million ?	79	28	5	82	28	6
b. What was the 1994 Fire department spending to nearest million ?	71	25	3	84	27	4
c. Which department spent nearly £6 million in 1994 ?	28	-	<1	36	2	-
LEVEL 2						
1. Two families go to a restaurant...						
a.. What is the total bill, including $12^{1/2}$% service charge ?	99	83	47	97	79	55
2. Details of credit schemes to buy furniture on...						
a. Which is the cheapest way of paying monthly ?	60	10	2	56	7	2
b. Which is the cheapest way of paying overall ?	64	14	1	61	11	2
c. And by how much cheaper is it overall ?	88	48	11	88	41	17
3. How much do people spend on food, fuel, shelter...						
a. What % of income spent on above if earn £10,000 per year ?	57	5	<1	54	4	2
b. What % of income does someone in USA spend if they earn £30,000 per year?	59	12	3	62	12	5
c. What relationship between earnings and cost of living does the graph show from 1993?	90	61	38	86	64	38
d. What is the % difference between the rise in earnings and the rise in cost of living in 1994?	82	47	19	87	56	26

Table A3
The Malaise Inventory, (Rutter et al, 1970)

	Yes (1 pt)	No (0 pts)
1) Do you often get back-ache?	☐	☐
2) Do you feel tired most of the time?	☐	☐
3) Do you often feel miserable or depressed?	☐	☐
4) Do you often have bad head-aches?	☐	☐
5) Do you often get worried about things?	☐	☐
6) Do you usually have great difficulty in falling or staying asleep?	☐	☐
7) Do you usually wake unnecessarily early in the morning?	☐	☐
8) Do you wear yourself out worrying about your health?	☐	☐
9) Do you often get into a violent rage?	☐	☐
10) Do people often annoy and irritate you?	☐	☐
11) Have you at times had a twitching of the face, head or shoulders?	☐	☐
12) Do you suddenly become scared for no good reason?	☐	☐
13) Are you scared to be alone when there are not friends near you?	☐	☐
14) Are you easily upset or irritated?	☐	☐
15) Are you frightened of going out alone or of meeting people?	☐	☐
16) Are you constantly keyed up and jittery?	☐	☐
17) Do you suffer from indigestion?	☐	☐
18) Do you suffer from an upset stomach?	☐	☐
19) Is your appetite poor?	☐	☐
20) Does every little thing get on your nerves and wear you out?	☐	☐
21) Does your heart often race like mad?	☐	☐
22) Do you often have bad pains in your eyes?	☐	☐
23) Are you troubled with rheumatism or fibrosis?	☐	☐
24) Have you ever had a nervous breakdown?	☐	☐

If 'Yes' is answered to 7 or more questions, a 'depressed' label is assigned

Faces behind the Figures

'Marcus'

Marcus has very low numeracy and average literacy skills. He acknowledges his difficulties with number tasks, and reports particular difficulties with using a calendar. Marcus left full-time education at 16, with 3 low grade C.S.E. passes. He has never been on a course to help overcome his difficulties. Marcus is registered disabled, having suffered an amputation, and receives state benefits. Since 1984 he has also worked for 3 hours a week, peeling potatoes in a local café, for £9. Marcus married his current partner in 1991, but has a 15 year old daughter from a previous relationship. He lives with his wife in local authority housing in the North. He finds it difficult to trust people, is quite argumentative, and was assessed with symptoms of depression.

'Janice'

Janice has very low literacy and average numeracy skills. She left full-time education at age 17, and has since attained a GNVQ3. Janice currently works part-time as a Personal Assistant, earning £121 per week, but has spent more than 13 years working on a full-time basis. Surprisingly, Janice has never had any work-related training, but has been promoted on at least two occasions. She lives in Yorkshire with her husband and two children. She married and had her first child at 21.

'Michael'

Michael also has very low literacy and numeracy skills. He left full-time education at 16 without any formal qualifications. He has always worked full-time, being a Painter and Decorator since 1991. Michael has never experienced a promotion and has received no work-based training. He earns £145 per week. Michael married at age 26, and has two children, his first at 29. Michael was assessed to be depressed but thought his life was just okay.

'Margaret'

Margaret has very low literacy and very low numeracy skills, but only reports difficulties with spelling. She left full-time education at age 16 with no formal qualifications. Margaret does not work and receives £130 per week in state benefits. She has only spent 4 years in full-time employment since she was 16. She is now long-term sick, and reports to be in generally poor physical health. On a scale of 0-10 for satisfaction with her life, Margaret reported '0'. Margaret was also assessed to be very depressed. She lives in rented accommodation in Wales with her own mother. Margaret is unmarried, and although she had two children in quick succession when she was 21, these children do not live with her.

'Daryl'

Daryl has very low literacy and numeracy skills. He left full-time education at 16 with 7 exam passes. He has spent over 20 years in full-time employment. He has never been promoted or been on a training course. He works more than 40 hours every week. From 1985 he has been employed as a Dyers Operative, and earns £170 per week. Daryl has never married and still lives with his parents in Yorkshire. He reports to be very satisfied with his life.

'Amanda'

Amanda has very low literacy and average numeracy skills. She left full-time education at age 16, with a couple of low grade C.S.E. passes. Amanda has only worked on a full-time basis for three years from the time she left school. Between 1986 and 1991 she worked part-time in a fruit and vegetable shop, earning just £37 per week. She left following the birth of her second child, and has since taken on a full-time home-care role. She lives in the North with her husband and two children. She had her first child at age 18, marrying when she was 19.

'Ronnie'

Ronnie has very low literacy and numeracy skills. Ronnie left full-time education at 16, and has no formal qualifications. He has spent less than 4 years in full-time employment over the years. He is out of the labour market with long-term health problems, and receives a variety of state benefits. Ronnie was married and has three children. This marriage has broken down and he currently lives with one of his daughters in Yorkshire.

'Louise'

Louise was assessed with very low numeracy and average literacy skills. She had no formal qualifications, and only reported spelling difficulties. From age 16, Louise had spent less than 4 years in full-time work, moving between part-time jobs and full-time home-care responsibilities. Between 1991-1993 she worked 14 hours a week as a Domestic Supervisor, and received £46. She has been unemployed since this time. Louise married when she was 20, and has two children, her first at 22. Louise's husband was also unemployed. They live in the North of England in local authority housing. She was quite satisfied with her life, but showed signs of depression.

'Brian'

Brian also has very low numeracy and average literacy skills, and is aware of his difficulties. Brian left full-time education at 16, has 5 examination passes. He has never been unemployed, and currently works full-time in a factory as a CNC Setter Operator. Brian has not been on any training courses, has never been promoted, and earns £190 per week. He has never married, and lives alone in the South East. He is buying his home, and thinks life is okay.

'Maureen'

Maureen did not think she had skills difficulties, but was assessed with a very low numeracy ability. She left full-time education at 16 with no formal qualifications. Maureen works for 23 hours a week as a Deputy Manageress in a shop, for which she receives £70. She has been on numerous training courses, and has been promoted on more than 2 occasions. Maureen married and had her first child at age 19. She had 6 children by the time she was 27. She lives in the North West of England in local authority housing with her husband (who is permanently sick, and receives state benefits) and their 4 youngest children. Maureen is quite satisfied with her life.

Sample Design and Response

Survey and Response

NCDS Sample Survey of Basic Skills

Peter Shepherd

Introduction

The fieldwork for the survey was conducted between 23 May and 7 July, 1995 by the MORI research organisation. This Appendix reports on the design, development and conduct of the survey; and reviews the extent and nature of survey response.

Survey Instruments

The survey instruments used were developed by SSRU and the survey contractor - MORI, in consultation with the Basic Skills Agency. There were three:

(a) *Literacy and Numeracy Assessments* - a new assessment based on development work undertaken on behalf of the Agency by the National Foundation for Educational Research.

(b) *Interview* - to obtain information about key aspects of the current social, economic and health circumstances of the cohort member; to update the job -, family - and housing - history information gathered during the fifth and latest major NCDS follow-up in 1991 - NCDS5; and to include the questions on self-reported basic skills problems used in earlier NCDS and BCS70 surveys.

(c) *Self-completion questionnaire* - to obtain other information about, for example, self-reported occupational skills, and attitudes. Again, this will update/repeat information gathered during NCDS5.

Pilot surveys

Two pilot surveys were undertaken:

1. *Literacy and Numeracy Assessment Pre-test*, 17-21 March - In total 21 interviews were conducted among a quota sample of respondents age 25-40 years in 4 sampling areas. All interviewers attended personal briefings and debriefings and both interviewers and respondents completed a short feedback questionnaire on the assessments. Twelve literacy and twelve numeracy assessments were piloted, taking an average of 27 and 21 minutes, respectively, to complete.

Following this pilot, and in consultation with the BSA, the number of individual assessment tasks was reduced to 19 (9 literacy and 10 numeracy), and elements of certain tasks modified or dropped.

2. *Pilot of all Interview, Self-completion, Assessments*, 8-18 April - In order to test all survey instruments and procedures, a total of 31 pilot interviews were conducted among a sample of NCDS cohort members in 5 postcode areas in SE England. Again, all interviewers attended personal briefings and debriefings. The modified literacy and numeracy assessments took an average of 24 and 18 minutes, respectively, while the interview averaged 37 minutes, and the self-completion 12 minutes.

As a result of this second pilot, changes were made to both the Assessments and the Interview, once again in consultation with the BSA.

The Assessments were further amended by reducing the number of assessments (to 8 literacy tasks and 9 numeracy tasks), and modifying elements of certain tasks (the three writing tasks were combined into one task covering three levels).

The Interview was amended by simplifying the treatment of employment and qualifications.

Copies of the instruments may be obtained from SSRU.

Fieldwork

Before beginning work on data collection, all 79 interviewers working on the project attended one of six personal briefings, held across the country in the period 22-30 May. The briefings provided: instructions on all aspects of the survey, including contacting procedures, survey instrument structure and content and required them to work through a dummy interview to ensure that they understood all sections of the instrument. Particular attention was given to the administration of the assessments, with all interviewers practising each of the tasks. A member of the SSRU team attended each of these briefings in order to give the background to the survey, answer queries, and to assure themselves that the selected interviewers were competent to administer all aspects of the survey, especially the assessments.

Copies of the interviewer instructions were supplied to all interviewers working on the survey. They may be obtained from SSRU.

All initial contact with cohort members made by interviewers was by telephone, or by visiting the cohort members' homes. This procedure was adopted to minimise non-response amongst cohort members with literacy difficulties. Interviewers were instructed to explain the purpose and nature of the survey, and to make an appointment to visit the cohort member's home at a convenient time. During this visit, the Interview and Self-completion were administered before the Assessments. Where cohort members experienced difficulty in answering the Self-completion, they were assisted by the interviewer. The interviewer also recorded the nature of any help given.

Analysis shows that the Interview took an average of 29 minutes to complete, the Self-completion some 5 minutes, and the Assessments an average of 35 minutes.

Sample Design

The sample for the NCDS 1995 Sample Survey was selected by replicating the sampling design adopted for the BCS70 21-year Sample

Survey - also funded by the BSA (then known as the Adult Literacy and Basic Skills Unit). Applying the same set of rules to draw a sample of NCDS cohort members. This provides a representative sample with a geographical distribution which reflects that of the NCDS cohort as a whole, and will be similar, but not the same as, that selected for the BCS70 Survey (see Ekinsmyth C and Bynner J, 1994).

The sample was drawn from the 10,851 cohort members living in England and Wales for whom SSRU had a current address in February 1995. It was designed to have the same regional distribution of cohort members as was observed in the population of all NCDS members living in England and Wales.

It is a clustered sample design, based on postcode areas. The postcode area is designated by the initial, non-numeric, part of the code. Twenty-five clusters were selected using interval sampling. An interval of 434 cohort members was used (25 x 434 = 10,851). The cumulative totals of cohort members living in each postcode area were listed. Postcode areas were listed in geographical order to approximately maintain their relative positions. Starting from a randomly selected point, postcode areas were chosen where they contained each 434th cohort member. If a selected postcode area contained too few cohort members to be viable, the next adjacent postcode area was also included in that cluster.

In order to maintain the original regional distribution, the number of cohort members selected in each of the chosen clusters was proportional to the total number of cohort members resident in the region containing that cluster. Where regions contained more than one selected postcode area, the distribution of sampled cohort members reflects the relative numbers of cohort members resident in those postcode areas. Cohort members were chosen at random within the selected postcode areas.

Table A1 shows the target and achieved distribution of the sample - each postcode area represents a cluster.

Table A1:
NCDS sample by Region and Postcode Area

Region	Postcode area	Planned sample n	Planned sample %	Interviews achieved n	Interviews achieved %
North		**111**	**6.72**	**122**	**7.12**
	NE	111	6.72	122	7.12
North West		**212**	**12.84**	**226**	**13.19**
	L	108	6.54	104	6.07
	LA	21	1.27	23	1.34
	OL	34	2.06	43	2.51
	WA	49	2.97	56	3.27
Yorkshire & Humberside		**176**	**10.66**	**184**	**10.74**
	DN	79	4.78	79	4.61
	LS	97	5.88	105	6.13
East Midlands		**110**	**6.66**	**117**	**6.83**
	DE	46	2.79	46	2.69
	LE	64	3.87	71	4.14
East Anglia		**70**	**4.24**	**76**	**4.44**
	NR	70	4.24	76	4.44
South East		**354**	**21.44**	**368**	**21.48**
	CM	97	5.88	98	5.72
	LU	45	2.73	47	2.74
	SL	54	3.27	49	2.86
	SO	76	4.60	80	4.67
	TN	82	4.97	94	5.49
Greater London		**197**	**11.93**	**202**	**11.79**
	BR	30	1.82	35	2.04
	CR	30	1.82	33	1.93
	IG	21	1.27	22	1.28
	SE	66	3.99	63	3.68
	WD	23	1.39	23	1.34
	EN	27	1.64	26	1.52
South West		**159**	**9.63**	**162**	**9.46**
	BH	50	3.03	52	3.04
	GL	77	4.66	77	4.50
	TR	32	1.94	33	1.93
Wales		**103**	**6.24**	**101**	**5.90**
	CF	103	6.24	101	5.90
West Midlands		**159**	**9.63**	**155**	**9.05**
	B	99	6.00	97	5.66
	ST	38	2.30	35	2.04
	WV	22	1.33	23	1.34
Total		**1,651**	**100**	**1,714**	**100**

Response

As Table A1 indicates, response to the survey was very good, and enabled the regional targets to be met in most instances. Further details are given in Table A2.

Overall, 1,714 cohort members were interviewed during the survey. This represents 80 percent of those whose details were issued to interviewers, and 88 percent of those traced. The main causes of non-response are refusals and moving home.

Table A2: Summary of survey response

Survey outcome	*Number*	*Overall percent*	*Percent of those traced*
Interview	1714	79.9	87.6
Refused	184	8.6	9.4
Ill/away	46	2.2	2.3
Incapable of interview	12	.6	.6
Moved from postcode area	28	1.3	-
Moved whereabouts unknown	103	4.8	-
No contact after 4 or more calls	48	2.2	-
Address vacant	8	.4	-
Address not found	2	.1	-
	2145	100.0	100.0

Response Bias

Although generally satisfactory response rates have been achieved, anything less than a perfect response raises the question of whether those who were interviewed and assessed were representative of the sampled population - in this case, the cohort members living in England and Wales for whom SSRU had a current address in February 1995. This issue has been explored by exploiting a possibility only available to longitudinal studies - to compare respondents to the target sample, and to the sampled population.

Comparison with the target sample

Comparison with the target sample has been restricted to consideration of the regional distribution.

Table A3 contrasts the regional distribution of the target sample and achieved sample, and gives the *percentage bias* for each region. The percentage bias indicates the extent of the departure of the achieved sample from the expected distribution and is calculated as follows:

(Achieved sample % - Target sample %) / Target sample %) x 100

A negative percentage bias indicates under-representation in the NCDS 1995 Sample Survey, and a positive percentage bias shows over-representation.

It is clear that, although the regional distribution of the achieved sample is broadly in line with that of the target sample, Greater London and regions in the west are somewhat under-represented, whilst northern and eastern regions are rather over-represented.

Table A3: Regional distribution of target and achieved samples compared

Region	Target sample %	Achieved sample %	% Bias
North	6.72	7.12	5.93
East Anglia	4.24	4.44	4.64
North West	12.84	13.19	2.75
East Midlands	6.66	6.83	2.51
Yorkshire & Humberside	10.66	10.74	.76
South East	21.44	21.48	.19
Greater London	11.93	11.79	-1.17
South West	9.63	9.46	-1.80
Wales	6.24	5.90	-5.49
West Midlands	9.63	9.05	-6.04

Target sample %	Percent in sample as drawn
Achieved sample %	Percent in achieved sample
% Bias	(Achieved sample %) / Target sample%) / Target sample %) x 100

Comparisons with the sampled population

Comparisons between the achieved sample and the sampled population have been extensive. They are based on variables selected from the earlier NCDS follow-ups. The variables chosen include many relating to demography, education, post-school education and training, literacy and numeracy problems, social and economic circumstances, financial problems, the family and relationships, housing and household, and health. A full list of variables used in this analysis is given in Table A4 on page 132. It may be noted that many of these variables have been included in similar analyses designed to explore differential attrition in the more recent NCDS follow-ups.

Table A4 contrasts the characteristics of the sampled population (NCDS cohort members living in England and Wales for whom SSRU had a current address in February 1995) and those of the achieved sample for the 1995 NCDS Sample Survey using the wide range of variables described above. Again, the percentage bias is reported for each variable, indicating the extent of the difference between the cohort and the sample. For this table percentage bias is calculated as follows:

   (Sample % - Cohort %)/Cohort %) x 100

   where: Sample % = Percent in achieved sample.
          Cohort % = Percent in NCDS cohort with
          confirmed address.

As before, a negative percentage bias indicates under-representation in the NCDS 1995 Sample Survey, and a positive percentage bias shows over-representation.

The analysis provides an important and encouraging insight into differential response. Absolute differences between the sampled population and the achieved sample are, on the whole, small and this is reflected in many of the figures for percentage bias. Nevertheless, small differences can result in a relatively large figure for percentage bias where the percentage in the sampled population is small. Levels of statistical significance are not reported, but it should be noted that in samples of this size, tests of statistical significance are sensitive to very small differences. In general, the achieved sample does not differ greatly from the sampled population.

Overall, it appears that those with low achievements and aspirations whilst at school are under-represented, as are those who have not pursued education and training since leaving school. Also under-represented are: those who are handicapped; those who have been "in care"; those with origins in the lower social classes; those who grew up in families with financial problems; and who have experienced poor housing conditions.

Perhaps not surprisingly, this picture is similar to that emerging from the analyses of differential response to earlier NCDS follow-ups. However, these earlier analyses also revealed a marked under-representation of members of the ethnic minority communities. This appears not to be the case for the current survey.

Finally, it is important to note that this analysis of differential response reveals that those who reported problems with basic skills during the last 1991 NCDS follow-up (NCDS5) are under-represented in the achieved sample for the current survey. This is not unexpected, but it is stressed that the absolute percentage differences are small.

Data preparation

Following completion, survey instruments were returned to MORI, who were responsible for a preliminary visual edit; followed by data entry; and a preliminary computer edit to check that data is valid (ie: for the main part single-coded, 0-9), and within range (ie: as specified in the survey instruments).

Unedited and edited data, together with all completed survey instruments, were subsequently passed to SSRU for further processing. This included:

(a)   Coding of occupation data using
       Computer-assisted Standard Occupational Coding -CASOC
       software developed by the University of Warwick.

(b)   Further computer editing to ensure that data is consistent.
       This will sometimes require reference to the original survey
       instruments to resolve problem cases.

(c)   ***Establishment of a clean and documented cross-sectional
       data base*** to facilitate early analysis.

(d)   Longitudinal linking of the new sample survey data with
       that from NCDS5 and earlier follow-ups to establish a
       longitudinal database to permit more detailed and
       longitudinal analysis. This included further checks
       on consistency.

Table A4:   Comparison of the NCDS Cohort and the 1995 Sample

	Source	Cohort %	Sample %	% Bias
Demographic Variables				
Male cohort members	ALL	49.8	46.8	-6.02
Mother born in West Indies	NCDS2	.7	.8	14.29
Father born in West Indies	NCDS2	.8	.8	.00
Child's ethnic group is Afro-Caribbean 11	NCDS2	.8	.7	-12.50
Ethnic identification Afro-Caribbean at 33	NCDS5	1.1	1.1	.00
Education				
Attended 3 or more schools 5-7	NCDS1	3.2	3.5	9.37
Attended 3 or more schools 5-11	NCDS2	15.7	17.0	8.28
Attended 3 or more schools 11-16	NCDS3	3.1	3.3	6.45
Attended comprehensive school 16	NCDS3	58.8	58.9	.17
Reading Test Score Low (<17) at 7	NCDS1	17.5	14.1	-19.43
Reading Test Score Low (<11) at 11	NCDS2	17.8	15.4	-13.48
Arithmetic Test Score Low (<4) at 7	NCDS1	26.4	24.3	-7.95
Mathematics Test Score Low (<7) at 11	NCDS2	18.0	16.8	-6.67
Teacher rates mathematics ability below average/poor at 16	NCDS3	30.8	26.9	-12.66

Continued...

	Source	Cohort %	Sample %	% Bias
Teacher rates English ability below average/poor at 16	NCDS3	21.1	17.7	-16.11
Parents don't want child to stay at school at 7	NCDS1	3.9	3.4	-12.82
Mother shows little interest in child's education at 7	NCDS1	13.6	11.5	-15.44
Father shows little interest in child's education at 7	NCDS1	14.6	12.4	-15.07
Father has little interest in child's education at 11	NCDS2	16.0	13.9	-13.12
Mother has little interest in child's education at 11	NCDS2	12.4	11.3	-8.87
Father shows little interest in child's education at 16	NCDS3	16.6	14.8	-10.84
Mother shows little interest in child's education at 16	NCDS3	15.2	12.7	-16.45
CM intends to leave school at 16 at 11	NCDS2	20.6	19.8	-3.88
Likely to leave school at 16 CM's view at 16	NCDS3	61.1	60.5	-.98
CM wants job on leaving school - view at 16	NCDS3	18.4	17.7	-3.80
Post-school Education and Training				
Left school at 16 or under	NCDS4	70.2	70.3	.14
No further education, training or apprenticeship by 23	NCDS4	14.4	11.9	-17.36
No qualifications by 23	NCDS4	51.3	51.7	.78
No qualifications by 33	NCDS5	11.0	10.8	-1.82
Taken any qualification courses by 33	NCDS5	33.9	34.5	1.77
Taken 3 or more qualification courses by 33	NCDS5	19.4	19.0	-2.06
Taken any work related training courses by 33	NCDS5	47.8	48.4	1.26
Done evening classes, etc "out of interest" by 33	NCDS5	34.5	34.4	-.29
Done more than 3 courses "out of interest" by 33	NCDS5	14.2	14.7	3.52

continued...

	Source	Cohort %	Sample %	% Bias
Literacy and Numeracy Problems				
Can't read enough to cope with everyday needs (teacher's view) at 16	NCDS3	1.1	.5	-54.55
Child can't do calculations required by an everyday shopper (teacher's view) at 16	NCDS3	2.1	1.8	-14.29
Problems with reading since 16 reported at 33	NCDS5	4.2	3.6	-14.29
Attended courses/class to improve reading reported at 33	NCDS5	17.0	16.7	-1.76
Writing/spelling problems since 16 at 33	NCDS5	9.8	9.3	-5.10
Problems with numbers/arithmetic since 16 reported at 33	NCDS5	3.0	2.6	-13.33
Attended any courses/class to improve numberwork by 33	NCDS5	9.3	6.7	-27.96
Any reading/writing/spelling/ numberwork problem by 33	NCDS5	9.5	9.3	-2.11
Social and Economic Circumstances				
Father stayed at school after minimum leaving age	NCDS1	24.0	23.1	-3.75
Father's social class at birth - Manual	PMS	79.3	79.8	.63
Father's social class 1965 - Manual	NCDS1	64.7	63.7	-1.55
Father's social class at 11 - Manual	NCDS2	62.4	61.4	-1.60
Father's social class at 16 - Manual	NCDS3	60.5	59.2	-2.15
Cohort Member's social class at 23 - Manual	NCDS4	42.7	41.8	-2.11
Cohort Member's social class at 33 - Manual	NCDS5	37.8	36.7	-2.91
Employed at 23	NCDS4	75.3	76.8	1.99
Employed at 33	NCDS5	79.7	78.3	-1.76
Five or more jobs by 23	NCDS4	14.6	14.0	-4.11
Five or more jobs 33	NCDS5	16.4	15.4	-6.10

continued...

	Source	Cohort %	Sample %	% Bias
Financial Problems				
Receiving free school meals at 11	NCDS2	9.0	7.8	-13.33
Receiving free school meals at 16	NCDS3	8.5	7.1	-16.47
Family had serious financial hardship in last year at 11	NCDS2	10.0	10.3	3.00
Family had serious financial trouble in last year at 16	NCDS3	9.0	8.7	-3.33
Ever been 2 months or more behind with rent/mortgage at 33	NCDS5	7.7	7.5	-2.60
Cohort Member/Partner receiving state benefit at 33	NCDS5	71.8	73.7	2.65
Cohort Member/Partner receive other regular income at 33	NCDS5	10.5	10.0	-4.76
Cohort member/Partner have savings at 33	NCDS5	79.8	81.8	2.51
Cohort Member/Partner have investments at 33	NCDS5	30.9	29.2	-5.50
Cohort/Partner have debts at 33	NCDS5	34.7	36.7	5.76
Family and Relationships				
Child ever in care by 16	NCDS3	3.1	2.2	-29.03
With natural mother at 7	NCDS1	97.5	97.8	.31
Natural mother at 11	NCDS2	96.7	96.6	-.10
Natural mother at 16	NCDS3	95.4	95.2	-.21
Parents ever permanently separated/ divorced by 33	NCDS5	15.1	14.6	-3.31
Married at 23	NCDS4	44.7	45.6	2.01
Has partner (spouse/cohabitee) at 33	NCDS5	80.1	81.9	2.25
Children at 23	NCDS4	23.5	23.8	1.28
Has children at 33	NCDS5	69.0	71.0	2.90

continued...